THE
WOMEN OF TORQUE :
(THE FORCE HISTORY CHOSE TO FORGET)

THAAVASMI ORIGINALS

Written by

N.VIVEK REDDY

(ARJUN)

Contents:

****

Book is dedicated to shri Radha-krishna

*Jai shree krishna & Jai Jagannatha *

"*Beauty is a concept that has fascinated humanity across cultures and eras. While beauty exists in countless forms, each unique and incomparable, the divine beauty of Radharani stands beyond worldly measures. Her beauty is not just physical but also spiritual, radiating love, grace, and devotion. It is an ethereal charm that transcends material comparisons, making her an eternal symbol of divine love and beauty.*"

ABOUT THE BOOK

Bhagavad Gita Chapter 10, Verse 34 (Shloka 10.34)

"mṛtyuḥ sarva-haraś cāham udbhavaś ca bhaviṣyatām |

kīrtiḥ śrīr vāk ca nārīṇāṁ smṛtir medhā dhṛtiḥ kṣamā ||"

Translation:

"I am death, the all-devouring, and I am the origin of all that shall be. Among women, I am fame, prosperity, speech, memory, intelligence, steadfastness, and patience."

This sloka influenced me a lot to write this book as society with few selfish people made women contribution to be kept behind the curtains and the actual contributions were buried.

History is often incomplete, shaped by the perspectives and priorities of those who recorded it. In this process, many stories have been overlooked or forgotten—especially those of women. Indian women, in particular, have played significant roles across different eras, yet their contributions have not always been given due recognition. This book is an attempt to bring these narratives to light, offering a broader and more balanced understanding of the past.

From ancient civilizations to the modern world, women have been philosophers, leaders, warriors, and innovators. While some aspects of history highlight challenges like sati, dowry, and social restrictions, there also exist accounts of Vedic scholars, medieval rulers, and reformers who influenced the course of history in profound ways. By exploring both the struggles and the achievements, this book aims to present a comprehensive view of women's place in Indian history.

Through eighteen chapters, this book will take you on a journey across time—from the early societies and the Vedic period to the women of medieval India, from the reformers and revolutionaries of the colonial era to the changemakers of modern times. It is not an attempt to rewrite history but to bring forth stories that have long remained in the background.

This is a study of the women of torque—those whose strength and influence helped shape the world, even when history chose to forget them.

ABOUT THE AUTHOR

N. Vivek Reddy is an author, historian, and researcher with a deep interest in history, technology, economics, and societal transformations. His work focuses on exploring overlooked narratives, analyzing historical patterns, and providing fresh perspectives on contemporary issues.

He has written several books, including "The Art of Warrior Serenity Z," which is based on real-life experiences and includes insights into the education system. His fascination with history led him to author a comprehensive study on Rajput history, bringing to light the valor and legacy of Rajput dynasties. Additionally, he has written a book on Elon Musk's biography and his contributions during Trump's era, examining the intersection of technology, business, and political influence. Beyond books, he actively publishes academic papers on history and economics, contributing to scholarly discussions.

In The Women of Torque: The Force History Chose to Forget, N. Vivek Reddy presents a well-researched and balanced exploration of women's contributions across different eras, particularly in India. By bringing forward stories that have long remained in the background, he challenges misconceptions and highlights the often-overlooked role of women in shaping civilizations.

CHAPTER -1
THE HIDDEN
HALF OF HUMANITY

The Hidden Half of Humanity: How Narratives Shape History and Half-Knowledge Misguides Generations

History is not just a collection of dates and events—it is the foundation upon which we build our identities. But what happens when history is incomplete? When entire sections of society are erased or misrepresented?

For centuries, the role of women in history has been downplayed, misunderstood, or rewritten to fit prevailing narratives. Many of us have been taught that women were always subordinate, always passive, always waiting for change rather than driving it. But is this the full story? Or is it just a carefully crafted illusion, built on selective memory and misinterpretation?

This book is an attempt to unearth the missing pieces—to go beyond the well-known struggles and uncover the strength, resilience, and influence of women who shaped civilizations. It is not about painting an overly romanticized past, nor is it about ignoring the real challenges women faced. Rather, it is about balance—about reclaiming the stories that were lost, hidden, or deliberately altered.

Women in Prehistory: The Forgotten Sapien

When we think of prehistoric humans, the image that often comes to mind is that of men hunting mammoths and women gathering berries. This idea, so deeply ingrained in our minds, was not based on archaeological evidence but on the assumptions of 19th-century scholars who projected their own patriarchal views onto the past.

However, newer discoveries challenge this outdated perception. Studies show that women in hunter-gatherer societies played active roles in hunting, tool-making, and decision-making.

• Peruvian burials have revealed women buried with hunting tools, suggesting they were not just gatherers but also warriors and hunters.

• The Kung people of Africa—one of the few remaining hunter-gatherer societies—demonstrate that women were not confined to domestic roles but participated equally in survival activities.

• Archaeological evidence from South America and Europe shows that prehistoric women had strong, muscular builds, indicating they engaged in physically demanding tasks.

So why were these contributions erased? The answer lies in the biases of those who recorded history. Prehistoric women were not weak, but their stories were buried beneath centuries of misinterpretation.

From Egalitarian Societies to Structured Patriarchy

Early human societies were surprisingly egalitarian. Both men and women played critical roles, and power structures were not as rigid as they later became. However, with the shift from hunter-gatherer lifestyles to agriculture, societies changed.

• Land ownership created hierarchies, leading to wealth accumulation and inheritance systems that favored men.

• Religious and legal codes began to define women's roles more rigidly.

• Physical strength became a measure of dominance, sidelining intellectual and strategic contributions.

But was patriarchy an inherent part of civilization? Not necessarily. Many ancient cultures maintained strong traditions of female leadership and respect for feminine power, even as societal structures evolved.

Ancient India: The Misunderstood Legacy of Women

India has often been portrayed as a land of female oppression—where women were confined, restricted, and subjugated. But the reality is far more complex. While oppression certainly existed, so did empowerment, agency, and reverence for women.

Women in Vedic India – A Society of Balance

The Vedic period (1500–500 BCE) was one of the most intriguing phases of Indian history. Women were not only respected but actively contributed to society as scholars, warriors, and spiritual leaders.

• Gargi and Maitreyi—two of the greatest philosophers of the time—engaged in intellectual debates with sages.

• Lopamudra, a Vedic scholar and wife of Rishi Agastya, composed hymns in the Rigveda.

• Women had the right to education (Vidya), the right to choose their own husbands (Swayamvara), and the right to property (Stridhana).

This was a time when the concept of Shakti (divine feminine power) was deeply embedded in cultural consciousness. Women were seen as the embodiment of wisdom, strength, and creation.

Chronicle Women: Strength Beyond the Stereotypes

Indian chronicles—often misinterpreted—tell stories of incredibly powerful women who shaped history:

• Sita (Ramayana) — Far from the helpless victim she is often portrayed as, Sita was a symbol of unshakable resilience and moral strength. Her decision to walk into the fire (Agni Pariksha) was not submission but a statement of her purity and autonomy.

• Draupadi (Mahabharata) — The queen of the Pandavas, Draupadi was no mere damsel in distress. She was sharp-witted, politically astute, and bold enough to challenge the most powerful men of her time. Her vow for justice led to the greatest war in Indian history.

• Goddess Aditi — Revered in the Vedas, Aditi was the primordial force of the universe, the mother of all celestial beings. She symbolized freedom, boundlessness, and the nurturing yet fierce aspect of femininity.

• Rani Durgavati and Rani Abbakka — Warrior queens who fiercely resisted foreign invasions, proving that Indian women were not just protectors of culture but also defenders of their lands.

Yet, these women's legacies have often been reduced to mere footnotes in history books.

Colonial Misinterpretation: The British Lens on Indian Women

When the British arrived, they found an India that did not fit their preconceptions. While European women had limited rights, Indian women had been scholars, rulers, and business owners.

But instead of acknowledging this, British historians:

- Highlighted the worst aspects of Indian traditions while ignoring progressive ones.

- Used distorted narratives to justify colonial rule, portraying India as a place that needed "saving."

- Imposed Victorian gender norms, which ironically made women's conditions worse in many cases.

By the 19th century, many Indian customs that had once empowered women were weakened under colonial influence. The traditional education system, which had once included women, was dismantled. The space for female leadership shrank.

The Cost of Half-Knowledge: Generations of Forgotten Potential

For centuries, women were made to believe they had no legacy of power. This lack of historical representation created generations of self-doubt:

- "Women have always been weak."

- "Men and women were never equal."

- "Feminine power is a modern invention."

These falsehoods became self-fulfilling prophecies, forcing women to fight for rights they had once possessed. When history is misrepresented, identities are lost.

Rewriting the Narrative: A Balanced Perspective

This book is not about glorifying the past or ignoring historical injustices. It is about restoring balance.

- *Yes, women faced oppression, but they also led revolutions.*

- *Yes, societies restricted them, but many also revered them as goddesses.*

◦ *Yes, history was written by men, but it is now being rewritten by truth-seekers who refuse to accept one-sided narratives.*

Women were never weak. Their strength was just hidden.

Chapter-2
THE FIRST FEMINIST SOCIETY

The First Feminist Society

For centuries, we have been taught that equality is a modern concept—something mankind fought for, something that came after revolutions, struggles, and reformations. We have been told that gender rights, the recognition of diverse identities, and the rejection of rigid hierarchies are ideas of recent origin. And yet, if we look far enough into history, beyond the ruins and the dust that has settled over ancient civilizations, we find something remarkable. We find a civilization that, thousands of years ago, had already mastered what we still strive for today—a society that flourished without oppression, where women were central to daily life, where gender was fluid, and where violence was not the foundation of power.

This civilization, buried under time and mystery, was the Indus Valley Civilization. It spanned more than 680,000 square kilometers, covering what is now India, Pakistan, and Afghanistan, making it one of the largest and most advanced societies of its time. The people of the Indus Valley built cities that followed careful planning, with structured streets, water management systems, and uniform architecture that hinted at something revolutionary—a society that had no kings, no ruling class, no massive temples or palaces to establish power. And, more importantly, they left behind traces of a world where women were not just seen but honored, where sex was not a taboo, and where equality was not an aspiration but a reality.

The Evidence of Equality in Indus Valley Civilization

It is easy to romanticize the past, to paint ancient societies as utopias without proof. But the Indus Valley Civilization gives us evidence—concrete, undeniable, archaeological proof of its unique approach to life, gender, and power.

1. Women as Central Figures in Society

One of the most telling discoveries in Indus cities has been the terracotta figurines, unearthed from sites like Harappa, Mohenjo-daro, and Dholavira. These figurines, often of women, are not simply decorative objects but symbols of fertility, power, and prosperity.

Some figurines exaggerate female features—wide hips, full breasts, and detailed jewelry. This isn't just artistic expression; it suggests that women were seen as life-givers, central to both the household and the economy. Unlike other civilizations where women were often depicted in subordinate roles, these figurines show women standing tall, elaborately adorned, holding objects of importance, indicating that they may have held positions of authority. A study by Jithin R. Veer in "A Glimpse at the Human Figurines of the Indus Valley Civilization" notes that these figurines might not just represent fertility but also prosperity and leadership, a departure from the typical image of passive womanhood found in later patriarchal societies.

2. Jewelry and Economic Status

The Indus Valley people were skilled artisans and traders, and jewelry was a significant part of their material culture. But what stands out is how much of this jewelry was associated with women. Excavations have uncovered necklaces, chokers, bangles, and elaborate headdresses, similar to those seen on the figurines. This suggests that women had access to wealth and luxury, not just as possessions of men but as individuals of status themselves. Some scholars argue that women in Harappan society might have participated in trade, as evidenced by the discovery of female figurines near pottery workshops and faience production centers. The use of lost-wax casting for bronze sculptures, typically a high-skill craft, suggests that women were either artisans or symbols of the craftsmanship itself.

3. Recognition of Gender Fluidity

Perhaps one of the most striking aspects of Indus society is its apparent acknowledgment of more than two genders. A mysterious seal from Harappa, now housed in the National Museum of Karachi, depicts a human figure with a double-bun hairstyle, standing in front of a tiger. Scholars are divided on its interpretation.

Some believe it represents a deity, while others suggest it may be an early representation of a third-gender figure or a spiritual leader of ambiguous identity. The lack of rigid gender roles in Indus artifacts and art forms indicates that gender was not as strictly policed as in later societies.

4. A Society Without Kings or Wars

Unlike the great civilizations of Mesopotamia and Egypt, where rulers built pyramids and palaces to assert their dominance, the Indus Valley Civilization shows no signs of monarchy, organized priesthood, or centralized military control. The absence of royal tombs, grand temples, or conquest records suggests a decentralized, possibly democratic society. Unlike

Mesopotamian or Egyptian societies, where women's power was mostly limited to noble or divine status, Indus women might have been part of governance and decision-making structures. A study by Rita P. Wright in "The Ancient Indus: Urbanism, Economy, and Society" argues that Indus society may have operated on collective decision-making rather than a hierarchical system, allowing for greater gender parity.

5. Sexuality Was Not a Taboo

One of the most intriguing aspects of Indus culture is its openness about sexuality. Unlike later societies that imposed rigid moral codes, the Indus people seemed to embrace sex as a natural, even sacred, part of life. Many figurines depict explicit sexual themes, suggesting that sexuality was not something hidden or suppressed but celebrated. Some scholars argue that the "Dancing Girl" figurine of Mohenjo-daro, with her confident stance and arm adorned with bangles, represents more than just artistry—it symbolizes a woman comfortable in her identity, strength, and perhaps even sensuality.

Indus Valley Civilization Versus Other Ancient Civilizations

Unlike the Mesopotamian and Egyptian civilizations, where social hierarchies were rigid and power concentrated in the hands of a king or pharaoh, the Indus Valley Civilization appears to have functioned without an absolute ruler. In Mesopotamia, power was held by kings and priests who dictated laws and controlled large temple economies, while Egypt revolved around the pharaoh, a god-king who was the center of both political and religious life. The Indus people, however, left behind no evidence of monarchy, no grand palaces, and no records of conquests, suggesting that their society may have been governed by community decisions rather than centralized power.

The role of women in the Indus Valley also contrasts starkly with these civilizations. In Mesopotamia, women were largely confined to household roles, and while some priestesses or noblewomen wielded influence, the general structure was patriarchal. Egyptian women enjoyed more legal rights than their Mesopotamian counterparts, but they still operated within a society where men controlled wealth, politics, and religion. Indus women, on the other hand, were depicted in powerful positions, associated with wealth, fertility, and possibly even governance, making their status more advanced in terms of gender equality than that of their contemporaries.

Sexuality, too, was treated differently. While Mesopotamian and Egyptian texts often associated sex with religious rituals or used it as a tool of social control, the Indus Valley artifacts suggest a culture that openly embraced human relationships. The lack of punitive records or strict moral codes related to sex further supports the idea that the Indus people did not view sexuality through the lens of sin or repression.

And so, as we attempt to understand this civilization, we must acknowledge that what we consider "progressive" today was already a lived reality thousands of years ago. The Indus Valley Civilization was not just an advanced urban society; it was a society that had already achieved what we continue to struggle for—a world where power was shared, where gender did not dictate destiny, and where humanity was embraced in its fullest form.

A man might look upon this history and wonder—have we truly advanced, or have we simply strayed from the wisdom once known? Have we spent centuries creating barriers that this civilization never needed? We speak of equality as a modern ideal, yet the ruins of Harappa whisper a different truth. The people of the Indus Valley had already built a world where women were central, where gender was fluid, where no single ruler dictated the fate of millions.

Perhaps rather than moving forward, we are simply trying to reclaim what was once already known—the wisdom of the first feminist society.

Source: Image is taken from wonderlists.com

Chapter –3

THE ERA OF TRUE EMPOWERMENT

– VEDIC AGE

The modern world often debates women's empowerment as if it were a new concept. However, history tells us a different story. The Vedic age, one of the earliest and most intellectually advanced periods in Indian civilization, held women in high regard. They were not just respected but actively participated in various fields—education, warfare, governance, trade, and spiritual discourse. The notion that women were merely confined to domestic roles is a later distortion, far from the ideals of Vedic society.

This chapter explores the status of women in the Vedic period, drawing from primary sources such as the Rig Veda, Yajur Veda, Atharva Veda, Manusmriti, Brihaddharma Purana, and Ramayana, alongside historical evidence that reaffirms their role in shaping society.

1. Women as the Divine Manifestation of Power and Knowledge

1.1 The Feminine as the Supreme Force in the Universe

The concept of Shakti (divine feminine energy) is at the core of Vedic traditions. Unlike many cultures that positioned women as secondary, Vedic philosophy equated them with divinity itself.

• Rig Veda 10.125.3-5 (Devi Sukta)

"Aham Rudrebhir vasubhiś carāmyahamādityair uta viśvadevaih.

Aham mitrāvaruṇobhā bibharmyahamaham indrāgnī aham aśvinobhā."

Translation: "I move with the Rudras, the Vasus, the Ādityas, and all the gods. I uphold both Mitra and Varuṇa, Indra and Agni, and the Aśvins."

Meaning: This verse is spoken by the Goddess herself in the Rig Veda, declaring that she moves with the most powerful gods, ruling alongside them. This directly establishes that the feminine force (Shakti) is as powerful as the masculine, if not more.

• Durga Saptashati (Markandeya Purana, Chapter 5, Verse 16)

"Ya devi sarva-bhūteṣu buddhi-rūpeṇa saṃsthitā

Namastasyai namastasyai namastasyai namo namah"

Translation: "The Goddess who resides in all beings in the form of intellect, we bow to Her, we bow to Her, we bow to Her."

Meaning: Women were seen not only as nurturers but also as the bearers of supreme knowledge and intellect.

2. The Status of Women in Vedic Society

2.1 Social and Religious Status

- Manusmriti 3.56

"Yatra nāryastu pūjyante ramante tatra devatāḥ,

Yatraitāstu na pūjyante sarvāstatraphalāḥ kriyāḥ."

Translation: "Where women are honored, there the gods are pleased; where they are not honored, no sacred act yields rewards."

Meaning: This reinforces that a society's prosperity depends on the respect and dignity given to women.

- Brihaddharma Purana

Maharshi Vyasa declares:

"There is no better place of pilgrimage than the Ganges, no greater sustainer of the world than Lord Vishnu, no one as venerable as Lord Shiva, and no greater master than one's own mother."

Meaning: A mother's status is upheld as supreme, even above divine beings.

- Rig Veda 6.61.7

"A woman is the home, a woman is the mother, a woman is the daughter.

A woman is the bond that holds the family together."

Meaning: This verse acknowledges a woman's role as the foundation of society.

2.2 Women as Philosophers and Scholars

Women were not restricted from intellectual pursuits in the Vedic period. They participated in Shastrarthas (philosophical debates) and composed hymns found in the Vedas.

• Gargi Vachaknavi debated with Yajnavalkya in the Brihadaranyaka Upanishad, asking deep metaphysical questions about existence.

• Maitreyi, a philosopher and the wife of Yajnavalkya, was recognized for her wisdom in spiritual matters.

2.3 Women in Marriage and Family Life

The concept of marriage in Vedic times was based on companionship rather than subjugation. The seven vows (Saptapadi) of Hindu marriage reinforce the equality between husband and wife.

1. First Vow: Together, we will ensure food and nourishment.

2. Second Vow: We will develop physical, mental, and spiritual strength.

3. Third Vow: We will earn and manage wealth together.

4. Fourth Vow: We will share our joys and sorrows equally.

5. Fifth Vow: We will raise our children with morals and wisdom.

6. Sixth Vow: We will remain loyal to each other.

7.Seventh Vow: We will remain best friends and life partners forever.

This shows that Vedic marriages were based on mutual respect rather than a patriarchal hierarchy.

3. Women as Warriors and Leaders

3.1 Women Warriors

• Vishpala (Rig Veda 1.116.15)

Vishpala was a warrior queen who lost her leg in battle. The Asvins, divine physicians, provided her with an mechanical leg, allowing her to return to war. This proves that women were active on the battlefield.

• Sita and Shabari (Ramayana)

• Sita was not just a devoted wife; she was a strong, independent figure who upheld dharma.

• Shabari, a tribal woman, was revered by Lord Rama, demonstrating that women from all backgrounds held wisdom and spiritual authority.

3.2 Women in Governance and Administration

Historical sources confirm that Vedic women participated in governance:

• Aditi, mother of the Devas, was regarded as a cosmic ruler.

• Women were part of political discussions and royal decisions, as seen in the Sabha (assembly) system.

4. Women in Professions: Beyond the Domestic Sphere

4.1 Fields Where Women Excelled

• Agriculture and Animal Husbandry: Women managed cattle, farmlands, and irrigation.

• Weaving and Spinning: A major industry where women dominated.

• Trade and Commerce: Women engaged in local and international trade.

• Religious Functions: Women acted as priestesses (Brahmavadinis).

• Healing and Medicine: Ancient Ayurveda mentions female physicians.

• Education and Learning: Women composed hymns in the Vedas.

5. Vedic Views on Abortion and Contraception

Unlike later periods, the Vedic age had a pragmatic approach toward reproductive rights.

• Atharva Veda 6.11.3 mentions herbal remedies used as contraceptives.

• Charaka Samhita records early knowledge of abortion methods in cases of medical necessity.

This suggests that women had autonomy over their bodies, a stark contrast to the restrictions imposed in later times.

Conclusion

The Vedic age was an era of true empowerment, where women were not just protected but actively participated in every aspect of life—spiritual, intellectual, economic, and political. They were warriors, sages, traders, rulers, and scholars. Their status was not a privilege but a right, enshrined in the very fabric of Vedic thought.As we move forward, recognizing the wisdom of the past might be the key to shaping a more balanced future. Women were never weak; they were forces of nature. And history, when seen through the right lens, confirms this truth.

Social and Religious Status

• Equal Status in Society: Women were considered integral members of society, participating in domestic, religious, and even state affairs.

• Freedom in Marriage: Women had the right to choose their husbands (Svayamvara). Love marriages (Gandharva Vivaha) were accepted.

• No Dowry System: The concept of dowry (Stridhan) was meant to provide financial security to women, not burden their families.

• Independent Property Rights: Women could own, inherit, and manage property, as mentioned in Rig Veda (3.31.1).

• Religious Participation: Women performed Vedic rituals and were Brahmavadinis (female scholars of the Vedas).

2. Education and Intellectual Contributions

2.1 Women as Scholars and Philosophers

• Rig Veda (10.85.46) encourages women to study and gain knowledge.

• Atharva Veda (11.5.18) emphasizes education for women, stating that educated women create a strong foundation for society.

• The Taittiriya Upanishad records that women were taught alongside men in Gurukuls.

2.2 Women as Teachers

Women not only studied but also taught scriptures and philosophy.

• Lopamudra: A philosopher and wife of Sage Agastya, she composed hymns in the Rig Veda.

• Gargi Vachaknavi: She debated Yajnavalkya in the Brihadaranyaka Upanishad, questioning the nature of existence.

• Maitreyi: A scholar who discussed the philosophy of self and reality with her husband Yajnavalkya.

Shloka (Brihadaranyaka Upanishad 2.4.2)

"Maitreyi uvacha: Yenāham nāmṛtā syāṁ kimahaṁ tena kuryām?"

Translation: "Maitreyi asked: If wealth does not make me immortal, what shall I do with it?"

This demonstrates her deep understanding of spiritual matters.

3. Women Sages and Their Role in Religious Discourse

Women were not only participants in religious debates but were also revered as sages (Rishikas). Several composed hymns in the Rig Veda.

3.1 Prominent Women Rishis (Sages)

- Gargi Vachaknavi: A leading philosopher who questioned the concept of Brahman (the ultimate reality).

- Lopamudra: A poet and philosopher, credited with composing Rig Veda 1.179.

- Apala: A sage who composed Rig Veda 8.91, focusing on healing and Ayurveda.

- Vishwavara: A Vedic scholar who composed Rig Veda 5.28, highlighting cosmic order.

- Romasha and Shashwati: Women sages mentioned in the Vedas who contributed to philosophical thought.

Shloka (Rig Veda 10.39.7)

"Imam me gathinam brahma pavamani shravaya sakhi"

Translation: "O friend, hear my song of divine knowledge and wisdom."

This verse, attributed to Vishwavara, emphasizes that women had the authority to preach wisdom.

3.2 Women in Vedic Rituals

Women actively participated in yajnas (rituals). Some notable examples include:

- Goddess Savita performed the Ashwamedha Yajna (horse sacrifice).

- Sulabha Muni, a female sage, was known for her knowledge of dharma.

Atharva Veda (14.1.20) states: "A wife should be equal to her husband in knowledge and learning."

4. Historical Figures and Famous Personalities

Women played crucial roles in different spheres of life, from governance to warfare.

4.1 Women in Administration and Politics

- Aditi: Considered the mother of gods (Devas), Aditi is a powerful symbol of divine feminine authority.

- Kaikeyi (Ramayana): Though controversial, she was an accomplished charioteer and skilled in warfare.

- Shabari (Ramayana): A revered tribal woman who attained spiritual wisdom and was visited by Lord Rama.

4.2 Women as Warriors

- Vishpala (Rig Veda 1.116.15): A warrior queen who lost a leg in battle but was given an iron prosthetic by the Ashwini Kumaras.

- Mudgalani: Fought alongside her husband, Rishi Mudgala, in various conflicts.

Shloka (Rig Veda 1.116.15)

"Vishpala, the warrior queen, was granted an iron leg by the divine Ashvins, so she may continue to fight."

This proves that women were not just passive members of society but active warriors.

4.3 Women in Medicine and Healing

- Apala (Rig Veda 8.91): A healer and Ayurvedic expert.

- Kakshivati: A Vedic physician known for her medical knowledge.

4.4 Women in Trade and Commerce

- Ghosha (Rig Veda 10.39.7): A female merchant who participated in trade.

- Lopamudra: Apart from being a scholar, she was also involved in economic matters.

4.5 Women in Art and Music

- Shilabhattarika: A poet who composed works in Sanskrit.

- Vatsyayani: A famous musician from the Vedic period.

Final Thought:

The strength of a civilization lies in how it treats its women. The Vedic age stood as a testament to a society where women were not just respected but revered as the bearers of knowledge, power, and creation.

CHAPTER-4
THE ESSENCE OF HINDUISM-
WOMEN'S ROLE IN SHAPING TRADITIONS

Hinduism is not merely a religion but a living tradition, a philosophy that has endured for thousands of years. At its heart lies the balance of forces—the masculine and the feminine, the protector and the creator, the seeker and the nurturer. Unlike many religious traditions that place divinity solely in the male domain, Hinduism acknowledges a deeper truth: the cosmos itself is incomplete without the feminine force.

However, as history unfolded, the role of women in society underwent changes. While the Vedic age saw intellectual and spiritual equality, later centuries introduced restrictions, not because of Hinduism's core philosophy but due to external political and social upheavals. Repeated invasions, the turmoil of foreign rule, and the need to protect women from exploitation led to societal shifts that limited their freedoms. Yet, at its core, Hinduism has always recognized that women were not just participants in dharma but its very foundation.

The Divine Feminine: Shakti as the Supreme Power

From the earliest Vedic times, Hinduism has placed Shakti—the feminine energy—at the center of creation. Unlike traditions where goddesses are secondary to male deities, Hinduism asserts that even the mightiest gods derive their strength from the feminine:

• Shiva without Shakti is lifeless; he is "Shava" (a corpse).

• Vishnu, the preserver, depends on Lakshmi for prosperity and fortune.

• Brahma, the creator, cannot function without Saraswati, the goddess of wisdom.

This is not merely metaphorical but a spiritual reality. The Rig Veda itself declares through the Devi Suktam:

"I am the ruler, I am the upholder of dharma, I am the supreme power that moves through all gods."

This proclamation is not from a male deity but from the Goddess herself, emphasizing that power, wisdom, and sustenance are incomplete without the feminine divine.

Throughout history, Hinduism has revered independent goddesses—Durga, the warrior mother; Kali, the destroyer of ignorance; and Saraswati, the bestower of wisdom. Their worship continues to this day, proving that the feminine is not subservient but supreme.

Women as the Upholders of Dharma

Dharma, the force that sustains the universe, has never been the domain of men alone. In the Vedic period, women were scholars, philosophers, and spiritual guides. They were equal participants in intellectual discourse and religious life.

Women in Vedic Intellectual Traditions

The Upanishads and Vedic texts document women debating and challenging some of the greatest male sages:

• Gargi Vachaknavi questioned Sage Yajnavalkya on the nature of existence in the Brihadaranyaka Upanishad.

• Maitreyi, wife of Yajnavalkya, rejected wealth and declared that true fulfillment lay in knowledge, not material possessions.

Such records dispel the myth that women in Hinduism were ever considered intellectually inferior. In fact, their participation was so integral that women had their own Vedic hymns (Rishikas like Lopamudra, Apala, and Vishwavara composed verses of the Rig Veda).

The Role of Women in Rituals and Marriage

Even in household traditions, Hinduism emphasized that a home where a woman was not respected was doomed to fail. The Manusmriti, often misinterpreted, actually declares:

"Where women are honored, there the gods reside."

This sentiment was also reflected in marriage. The Hindu wedding ceremony is not a transaction but a sacred partnership. The Saptapadi—the seven vows exchanged between husband and wife—symbolize equality and mutual responsibility:
1. Sharing prosperity – Supporting each other in life.
2. Strength in adversity – Standing together in hardships.
3. Ensuring stability – Pledging financial and emotional security.
4. Preserving harmony – Strengthening family values.
5. Raising and educating children – A shared duty.
6. Wishing for longevity – Caring for each other's health.
7. Eternal companionship – A vow of unwavering devotion.
Unlike in some traditions where women were given away in marriage as property, Hinduism elevates the bride, with the groom himself seeking blessings from his wife, acknowledging that his journey of dharma is incomplete without her.

The Shift: Invasions, Protection, and Later Restrictions
Despite this strong foundation of equality, history took a turn. Over centuries, with foreign invasions and cultural disruptions,

Hindu society changed—not due to religious philosophy but out of necessity.

Impact of Invasions on Women's Freedom

When waves of invaders entered India—whether they were Turks, Mughals, or later colonial powers—one of their most brutal tactics was the mistreatment of women. Mass abductions, forced conversions, and enslavement of women were common in times of war. To protect their daughters, sisters, and wives, Hindu society imposed stricter norms:

• The veiling of women (purdah) became widespread, not due to Hindu scriptures but as a defensive measure against invaders.

• Child marriage became prevalent to prevent young girls from being abducted.

• Women's mobility and education were restricted to keep them safe from foreign rule.

These were not religious doctrines but survival strategies, developed in an era of turbulence. They were reactions to an age where foreign rulers saw women as spoils of war. The once-open institutions that welcomed female scholars and sages had to retreat, prioritizing security over education.

The Bhakti Movement: Resurgence of Women's Voices

Despite these changes, Hinduism never lost its core ideals. The Bhakti movement (7th–17th centuries) saw women reclaiming their voices, defying social restrictions to express their devotion through poetry, music, and philosophy.

• Mirabai, a Rajput princess, abandoned royal life to dedicate herself to Krishna.

• Andal, a Tamil saint, composed hymns still sung today.

- Akka Mahadevi, a Kannada poet, renounced societal norms to seek Shiva.

These women challenged societal limitations, proving that Hinduism itself had not changed—only society had.

Conclusion: The Everlasting Truth of Hinduism

At its core, Hinduism has always upheld the balance of energies—the masculine and the feminine. The philosophy never sought to limit women, but historical circumstances led to changes in practice.

If history has sometimes forgotten the role of women, it is not because Hinduism diminished them, but because foreign invasions forced society into a defensive stance. But as the Bhakti saints, Vedic scholars, and warrior queens of India have shown—whenever women's rights were constrained, Hinduism found a way to restore balance.

The world may have changed, and societies may have imposed restrictions, but the essence of Hinduism remains unchanged. It has always recognized that:

- Without Shakti, there is no Shiva.
- Without Saraswati, there is no wisdom.
- Without Lakshmi, there is no prosperity.

A civilization that respects its women, honors its traditions, and upholds its dharma will always flourish. And Hinduism, in its truest form, has always known this truth.

CHAPTER-5

THE WORLD MOVEDFORWARD BUT DID WOMEN FOLLOW?

History is often narrated as the story of progress—of empires rising, civilizations advancing, and humanity pushing the boundaries of knowledge and power. But within this grand narrative lies a question that remains largely unexplored: as the world moved forward, did women truly remain in the background, merely watching as events unfolded?

For centuries, historical accounts suggested so. Women were cast as nurturers, caretakers, and silent witnesses to the course of civilization. Yet, when we step beyond these long-held notions and examine the evidence, a different story emerges—one where women were not passive observers but active participants, shaping the very foundations of society.

Breaking the Myth: The Role of Women in Prehistoric Societies

For a long time, the standard belief was that prehistoric societies followed a simple division of labor—men hunted, and women gathered. This assumption was not based on strong evidence but rather on interpretations influenced by later societal norms.

However, archaeological discoveries in recent years challenge this view. The discovery of a 9,000-year-old burial site in the Andes, where a woman was buried with hunting tools, is just one of many examples showing that women actively participated in hunting. Similar findings from Africa, Europe, and Asia suggest that early human communities were far more egalitarian than once thought.

Another overlooked contribution comes from prehistoric art. Hand stencils found in caves, such as those in El Castillo, Spain, were long assumed to have been made by men. Yet, scientific analysis of finger proportions indicates that many of these stencils were created by women. The first artists of human civilization were not only men, but also women, shaping early human expression and communication.

Beyond Biology: The Shared Responsibility of Raising the Next Generation

It is often assumed that parenting was an exclusive responsibility of women in early societies, but historical and anthropological evidence suggests otherwise. Among hunter-gatherer communities that survive today, such as the Aka people of Central Africa, men participate in childcare as much as women. These practices likely reflect how early human societies functioned— child-rearing was a shared responsibility rather than a strictly gendered role.

Beyond the home, women were deeply involved in structuring the social and economic fabric of their communities. From managing food resources to forming social alliances, they played a role that extended far beyond motherhood, contributing directly to the survival and stability of early human groups.

The First Steps Towards Civilization: Agriculture and Settlement

The development of agriculture marked one of the greatest turning points in human history. While men were traditionally credited with this advancement, a closer examination suggests that women played a foundational role.

As primary gatherers, women had deep knowledge of plant cycles, soil conditions, and food storage techniques. They were likely the first to experiment with planting seeds and domesticating crops. Excavations at sites such as Çatalhöyük in modern-day Turkey provide evidence that women were central to early agricultural practices, food production, and pottery-making, all of which were critical to the success of settled societies.

Yet, as agricultural societies became more structured, the roles of men and women began to diverge. The shift from small communities to large civilizations brought about new power structures—ones that increasingly limited women's roles outside the household.

Shifting Social Structures: How Civilizations Redefined Women's Roles

Early civilizations showed significant variation in how they treated women:

 • In Mesopotamian societies, women engaged in trade, owned property, and held religious and administrative roles.

 • In ancient Egypt, women could run businesses, initiate divorces, and even rule as pharaohs.

 • In early Vedic India, women like Gargi and Maitreyi actively participated in philosophical debates alongside men.

However, as these societies grew more complex, social hierarchies became stricter. Legal codes such as the Code of Hammurabi (Babylon, 1754 BCE) imposed formal restrictions on women's rights. In classical Greece, where democracy flourished for free men, women were largely confined to domestic spaces.

The Rise of Patriarchal Systems

The emergence of patriarchy was a gradual process. Early human communities were more cooperative, but as civilizations expanded, war and territorial control became central concerns.

With the rise of standing armies and state institutions, male-dominated leadership structures solidified.

Inheritance laws began favoring sons over daughters, and religious doctrines were interpreted in ways that reinforced male authority. Over time, these developments created rigid social norms that positioned women primarily within domestic roles, reducing their participation in public life.

The Decline of Women's Rights in Ancient India

In India, the early Vedic period reflected a more balanced society where women were respected for their intellectual and spiritual contributions. However, over time, various factors—political instability, foreign invasions, and shifting social norms—led to increasing restrictions on their roles.

Practices such as purdah (veiling) and sati (widow immolation) were not part of early Hindu traditions but emerged in response to the need for protection during periods of foreign invasions. While these customs were initially meant to safeguard women, they later became institutionalized as societal norms, limiting their freedom further.

Rewriting the Narrative: Modern Archaeology and New Discoveries

Archaeological findings in recent decades have begun to challenge outdated perceptions of history. Excavations at sites like Göbekli Tepe in Turkey suggest that women played significant roles in early religious and social structures. DNA analysis of Viking warrior burials has revealed that some of the most skilled fighters were women. In India, discoveries at Rakhigarhi, a major Harappan site, show evidence of women's involvement in trade and governance.

These findings are not isolated—they form a growing body of evidence that challenges long-held assumptions about women's roles in history. The reality is not that women were absent from history, but that their contributions were often overlooked or downplayed.

Conclusion: Restoring a Forgotten Legacy

The idea that women merely watched as the world moved forward is not supported by evidence. They were hunters, artists, farmers, traders, philosophers, and rulers. Their roles may have been diminished over time, but their impact on civilization remains undeniable.

As we uncover new historical truths, we are not creating a new narrative—we are simply restoring what has long been forgotten. The past cannot be changed, but the way we tell its story can, and must, evolve to reflect the contributions of all who shaped it.

My Observations :

If early societies had a more balanced structure between men and women, why did civilizations eventually lean toward a male-dominated system? In my view, much of this shift was shaped by how power, survival, and social structures evolved over time. As human groups expanded, leadership and control over land, resources, and external threats became defining factors in societal roles. Those who managed these aspects naturally gained influence, and over time, authority became concentrated in certain hands.

Another factor to consider is security. As settlements grew and conflicts increased, societies might have prioritized stability over individual freedoms. Women, being central to the continuity of families and communities, were gradually placed in more structured roles. What may have started as a measure to ensure protection eventually turned into rigid customs that limited their participation in wider societal affairs.

When it comes to parenting, the shift in responsibility toward women might have been more about social convenience than necessity. In early human groups, responsibilities were likely shared more equally. However, as agriculture developed and inheritance-based power structures took hold, societal norms increasingly associated women with domestic roles. This wasn't necessarily due to any inherent differences but rather the way societies chose to organize themselves over time.

The real question is whether these changes were an inevitable part of civilization's progression or if they were simply the result of choices that favored certain groups over others. Looking at history, it seems that power often seeks to preserve itself, and those in control shape narratives that justify their dominance. But modern discoveries challenge many of these long-held beliefs, revealing that women were not passive observers of history—they were active participants whose contributions were often overlooked.

CHAPTER-6
REWRITING ANCIENT INDIA'S WOMEN

History, as traditionally recorded, often reflects the perspectives and biases of its chroniclers. While the exploits of kings and conquerors dominate the annals, the remarkable contributions of women frequently remain overshadowed or omitted.Did these women not engage in battles? Did they not govern with wisdom? Did they not contribute to literature, medicine, and philosophy? Indeed, they did. Yet, as time progressed, their stories were marginalized.As a man delving into history, I am compelled to question: Was this omission deliberate? Was it a consequence of evolving societal norms? Or did male historians simply overlook the central roles women played?

This chapter endeavors to rectify that oversight, reclaiming the voices of India's forgotten women—from Vedic sages to warrior queens, from intellectuals to rulers—whose impacts on India's past are profound.

Pioneering Scholars and Philosophers

1. Maitreyi (circa 8th century BCE)

Maitreyi was a renowned philosopher during the later Vedic period, known

for her profound discussions on the nature of the self (Atman) and ultimate reality (Brahman). In the Brihadaranyaka Upanishad, she engages in a deep dialogue with her husband, sage Yajnavalkya, exploring the essence of immortality and consciousness. Maitreyi's intellectual pursuits highlight the significant role women played in the spiritual and philosophical domains of ancient India.

Gargi Vachaknavi (circa 7th century BCE)

Gargi was a prominent philosopher who participated in intellectual debates in King Janaka's court. Known for her probing questions on the nature of existence and the cosmos, she challenged the esteemed sage

Yajnavalkya, showcasing her formidable intellect and deep understanding of metaphysics.

Sulabha (date unknown)

Sulabha was a distinguished philosopher and yogini who engaged in a profound discourse with King Janaka of Mithila, as documented in the Mahabharata. Renouncing worldly possessions, she pursued a path of spiritual enlightenment, challenging prevailing norms by asserting that all individuals are equally capable of attaining liberation. Her debate with King Janaka emphasized the non-duality of the self and advocated for equality in spiritual pursuits.

Other prominent people are **karaikal Ammaiyar, ubhayabharati, akka Mahadevi, lalleshwari , Ganga sati, kanhopatra, Chandra bati.**

Contributors to Arts, Literature, and Society

1. Avvaiyar (circa 1st and 2nd century CE)

A celebrated Tamil poetess, Avvaiyar's literary works, such as "Aathichudi" and "Kondrai Vendhan," impart moral lessons and are integral to Tamil literature. Her compositions continue to influence Tamil culture and education.

2. Prabhavati Gupta (circa 4th century CE)

As a queen and the daughter of Chandragupta II, Prabhavati Gupta assumed regency after her husband's demise. Her administrative orders, documented in various inscriptions, reveal her active role in governance and state affairs.

3. Vijayabha (circa 7th century CE)

Serving as a provincial ruler under the Chalukya dynasty, Princess Vijayabha's governance indicates involvement in political administration during that era.

4. Shakuntala

A central figure in ancient Indian literature, Shakuntala's story is immortalized in Kalidasa's play "Abhijnanashakuntalam." Her tale of love, separation, and reunion has been a source of inspiration in Indian art, literature, and theater, symbolizing grace and resilience.

VALIANT WARRIORS AND LEADERS

1. Prabhavati Gupta (4th century CE):

• Prabhavati Gupta was the daughter of the powerful Gupta emperor Chandragupta II and was married into the Vakataka dynasty. After the death of her husband, Rudrasena II, she assumed regency on behalf of her minor sons. Her effective administration maintained stability and strengthened alliances between the Gupta and Vakataka dynasties, showcasing her diplomatic acumen.

Copper Coins issued by Prabhavatigupta

Queen Didda of Kashmir (10th century CE):

• Despite being physically disabled, Queen Didda ruled Kashmir with resilience and strategic prowess. Ascending to power as regent for her son and later her grandson, she eventually became the sole ruler. Didda navigated court intrigues, consolidated power, and maintained the kingdom's sovereignty against external threats, leaving a legacy of strong female leadership in a patriarchal society. also known as **The Catherine of Kashmir**

Rani Udayamati (11th century CE):

• Rani Udayamati, queen consort of King Bhima I of the Chaulukya dynasty in Gujarat, is renowned for commissioning the Rani ki Vav, an intricately designed stepwell in Patan. This architectural marvel, adorned with detailed sculptures, reflects her patronage of art and culture. The stepwell not only served as a water resource but also as a testament to the era's engineering and artistic excellence.

Rani Rudrama Devi (1259–1289 CE):

• One of the few reigning queens in Indian history, Rani Rudrama Devi ascended the throne of the Kakatiya dynasty in present-day Telangana. Trained in statecraft and military tactics from a young age, she adopted the male title "Rudradeva" to assert her authority. Her reign was marked by administrative reforms, fortification of her capital Warangal, and successful military campaigns that expanded and secured her kingdom.

Rani Padmini (Padmavati) (13th–14th century CE):

• Rani Padmini, the queen of Chittor, is celebrated in folklore for her beauty and valor. According to legend, when Sultan Alauddin Khilji besieged Chittor to capture her, she chose self-immolation (jauhar) along with other women to protect their honor. While historical evidence is debated, her story symbolizes courage and the Rajput ethos of honor and sacrifice.

Rani Karnavati of Garhwal (died 1640 CE):

• Known as the 'Nak-Kati Rani,' Rani Karnavati of Garhwal defended her kingdom against Mughal invasions. She famously ordered the noses of captured Mughal soldiers to be cut off as a message to Emperor Shah Jahan, showcasing her defiance and strategic acumen. Her leadership maintained the independence of Garhwal during a tumultuous period.

Rani Durgavati (1524–1564 CE):

• Born into the Chandela dynasty, Rani Durgavati became the queen of Gondwana through marriage. After her husband's death, she assumed the throne and proved to be an able administrator and warrior. Her reign saw the flourishing of arts and public works. Facing Mughal aggression under Emperor Akbar, she led her troops valiantly in battle and chose to end her life over surrender, epitomizing courage and honor.

Rani Chennabhairadevi (16th century CE):

• Dubbed the "Queen of Pepper," Rani Chennabhairadevi ruled over the coastal Karnataka region for over 54 years. She maintained a robust trade network, especially in pepper exports, and defended her territory against Portuguese aggression. Her reign is noted for diplomatic skill, military strategy, and fostering economic prosperity through trade.

Rani Abbakka Chowta (16th century CE)

Queen Abbakka Chowta of Ullal fiercely defended her small principality against Portuguese colonial forces. Utilizing guerrilla warfare tactics, she managed to repel multiple invasions, earning her a revered place in regional folklore. Her resistance is celebrated as an early example of anti-colonial defiance in Indian history

Rani Velu Nachiyar (1730–1796 CE):

• Queen Velu Nachiyar of the Sivaganga estate in Tamil Nadu was among the first Indian queens to wage war against British colonial powers. Fluent in multiple languages and trained in martial arts, she formed alliances with neighboring kingdoms and employed effective military strategies. Notably, she organized a suicide attack, using a human bomb to destroy a British arsenal, long before such tactics became widespread.

Rani Tarabai Bhonsle (1675–1761 CE):

• Maharani Tarabai was a pivotal figure in the Maratha Empire. Following the death of her husband, Rajaram I, she assumed regency on behalf of her minor son, Shivaji II, in 1700 CE. Tarabai is acclaimed for her leadership during a critical period when the Maratha Empire faced Mughal aggression. She led successful military campaigns, expanded Maratha territories, and maintained the empire's sovereignty against formidable challenges.

Kittur Rani Chennamma (1778–1829 CE):

• Born in Kakati, Karnataka, Rani Chennamma became the queen of Kittur. In 1824, she led an armed rebellion against the British East India Company in defiance of the Doctrine of Lapse, aiming to secure her kingdom's independence. Despite initial successes, she was eventually captured and imprisoned. Her bravery and resistance

made her one of the earliest Indian rulers to fight against British colonialism.

Rani Lakshmibai of Jhansi (1828–1858 CE)

Born as Manikarnika Tambe in Varanasi, Rani Lakshmibai became the queen of Jhansi in North India. Following her husband's death, she assumed leadership during a period of political unrest. In 1857, she played a pivotal role in the Indian Rebellion against British colonial rule, leading her troops with remarkable bravery. Her defiant stand and martyrdom have made her a symbol of resistance and courage in India's struggle for independence.

Rani Avantibai (1831–1858 CE)

Queen of the Ramgarh kingdom in central India, Rani Avantibai Lodhi ascended to power after her husband's demise. Facing British attempts to annex her territory under the Doctrine of Lapse, she organized a formidable resistance during the 1857 uprising. Leading

her forces personally, she engaged in guerrilla warfare against the British. Ultimately, to avoid capture, she chose to end her own life, and her sacrifice is remembered as a testament to patriotism and valor.

Maharani Ahilyabai Holkar (1725–1795 CE)

Born in the village of Chondi in Maharashtra, Ahilyabai Holkar became the ruler of the Malwa kingdom after her husband's death. Renowned for her administrative acumen, she developed Indore into a prosperous city and was a patron of arts and culture. Her reign is marked by numerous infrastructure projects, including roads, temples, and ghats across India, reflecting her commitment to public welfare and devotion.

Sethu Lakshmi Bayi (1895–1985 CE)

As the Regent Maharani of Travancore from 1924 to 1931, Sethu Lakshmi Bayi implemented significant social and educational reforms. She focused on modernizing education, promoting women's rights, and improving public health. Her tenure is noted for progressive policies, including the abolition of certain regressive taxes and the encouragement of women's education, laying the foundation for future advancements in the region.

Maharani Gayatri Devi (1919–2009 CE)

Born into the royal family of Cooch Behar, Gayatri Devi became the Maharani of Jaipur through marriage. Celebrated for her beauty and elegance, she was also a pioneering woman in Indian politics. In 1962, she was elected to the Lok Sabha, achieving a record majority. She founded schools, including the Maharani Gayatri Devi Girls' Public School in

Jaipur, advocating for women's education and empowerment throughout her life.

A Conversation with History: The Women Who Shaped India

As I sit down to write, I find myself speaking to history. I ask questions, and history answers—through the voices of women who shaped India's destiny.

Narrator: Were women always powerful in India's history?

History: More than powerful—they were creators, thinkers, warriors, and rulers. The idea that women were always suppressed is false. In the Vedic age, women like Gargi and Maitreyi debated philosophy in royal courts. Lopamudra composed hymns that are still recited today. Apala was a physician whose knowledge of herbs was unmatched. These women were intellectual pioneers. Later, queens like Ahilyabai Holkar, Rani Durgavati, and Rani Lakshmibai carried this legacy forward, proving that leadership was not just a man's domain.

Narrator: Let's start with the Vedic women. Who was Gargi?

History: Gargi was India's first great philosopher. She challenged the great sage Yajnavalkya in a debate about the nature of existence. When most feared to question the wise, she stood up and dared to ask: What is the ultimate reality? What lies beyond space and time? Even today, her debates are considered milestones in Indian philosophical thought.

Narrator: And Maitreyi?

History: Maitreyi was a scholar of the Upanishads, a thinker ahead of her time. When her husband, Yajnavalkya, offered her material wealth, she asked, Will this make me immortal? Instead of riches, she chose wisdom, proving that true power lies in knowledge, not possessions.

Narrator: What about women in science and medicine?

History: Apala was a Vedic physician, an expert in herbal medicine. The Atharvaveda mentions her curing diseases with plants and rituals. Similarly, Kahola and Romasha were scholars who contributed to early mathematics and astronomy. Women were not just caretakers of the home; they were caretakers of knowledge.

Narrator: But then came the queens—how did they carry forward this legacy?

History: The queens did not just inherit power; they fought for it. When invaders came, they took up swords. When injustice rose, they defied societal norms. From Rani Durgavati to Rani Chennabhairadevi, they proved that leadership was not about gender, but about courage.

Narrator: Rani Lakshmibai—what made her a legend?

History: She was not just a queen; she was a warrior. When the British attacked Jhansi, she led her army into battle, sword in hand. With her son strapped to her back, she rode fearlessly, refusing to surrender. Even in death, she remained unconquered, becoming a symbol of India's resistance.

Narrator: And Rani Avantibai?

History: She, too, fought the British, but her story is often forgotten. When her kingdom was threatened, she gathered an army and led them into battle. Even when all seemed lost, she chose death over surrender, proving that true warriors never bow down.

Narrator: Ahilyabai Holkar—she was not a warrior, was she?

History: No, but she was a builder of empires. She rebuilt temples, constructed roads, and brought prosperity to Malwa. Where others ruled with the sword, she ruled with wisdom and justice. Even today, the city of Indore flourishes because of her vision.

Narrator: Sethu Lakshmi Bayi—what did she do for India?

History: She was a modern reformer. At a time when women had little voice, she pushed for education, women's rights, and temple architecture in Travancore. She saw the value of science and progress, proving that a ruler's duty is to uplift, not just govern.

Narrator: And Maharani Gayatri Devi?

History: She was India's first royal to step into democracy. Instead of staying in the palace, she entered politics, fighting for education and women's empowerment.She revived traditional Rajasthani crafts, ensuring that India's art and culture survived modernization. She proved that queens are not just symbols of beauty, but of strength.

Narrator: What about art and culture? How did women shape that?

History: Women were the first storytellers, the first artists, the first dancers. In ancient India, temple dancers preserved our classical traditions. Queens like Ahilyabai Holkar and Sethu Lakshmi Bayi built temples and libraries that became centers of art. Poets like Mirabai challenged societal norms through devotional songs. Even today, we see their impact in Bharatanatyam, Odissi, and Kathak, which all have roots in women's artistic expressions.

Narrator: So, history tried to forget them?

History: It tried, but it failed. These women's voices echo in our hymns, our temples, our battlefields, and our cities. Their stories were never truly erased—they live on in every woman who dares to question, to lead, to fight, and to create.

As I close this conversation with history, I realize something: India was never just built by kings—it was built by its women, too. From the Vedic philosophers to the warrior queens, from the artists to the reformers, they all played their part. And as long as we remember them, they will never be forgotten.

Chapter-7
The impact of historical Biases

The Impact of Historical Biases on Women

History is often written by the victors, and in this process, many voices are forgotten or distorted. Women, despite their undeniable contributions to society, have frequently been subjected to historical biases that altered their roles, rights, and status. These biases have left a lasting impact on multiple sectors—education, health, economy, politics, law, and even cultural identity. While ancient Indian society, particularly during the Vedic era, saw women as intellectuals, warriors, and leaders, later interpretations and external influences reshaped their roles, often diminishing their rights and freedoms.

This chapter explores the sectors where historical biases affected women, analyzing their origins and consequences. It also addresses controversial topics such as Sati and child marriage, with an evidence-based approach to separate myth from reality.

1. The Decline of Women's Education

During the Vedic period, women had access to education and actively participated in intellectual discourse. Rishikas (female sages) like Gargi and Maitreyi engaged in philosophical debates with scholars. Women composed hymns in the Rigveda, proving their equal standing in knowledge and learning. However, over centuries, historical biases limited their access to education.

Key Factors Behind This Decline:

• Manusmriti Misinterpretation: The Manusmriti, often blamed for restricting women's education, originally had verses advocating women's respect. However, later interpolations justified keeping women away from scholarly pursuits.

• Medieval Invasions: With the onset of foreign invasions (from Ghaznavids to Mughals), education for women was discouraged due to security concerns, as scholars feared kidnappings and forced conversions.

• Colonial Impact: British rule further deepened the problem by neglecting women's education in initial policies. Only in the late 19th and 20th centuries did reformers like Savitribai Phule revive female literacy efforts.

Proof and Modern Consequences:

• Census records from colonial India indicate a stark decline in female literacy compared to ancient India, reinforcing that this shift was imposed rather than natural.

• Even today, UNESCO data shows that female literacy rates in many parts of India lag behind male literacy, an outcome of centuries of systemic bias.

2. The Deterioration of Women's Health Rights

Ancient Indian medical texts like the Charaka Samhita and Sushruta Samhita discuss women's healthcare in depth, proving that female health was once a priority. However, historical biases altered medical priorities.

Causes of Decline:

• Shift in Social Structures: As patriarchal norms deepened, women's health became secondary to household duties.

• Colonial Neglect: British medical institutions did not initially cater to women, worsening the situation.

• Superstitions and Taboos: Menstruation and childbirth, once treated with scientific understanding in Ayurveda, were stigmatized, leading to harmful traditional practices.

Proof and Modern Consequences:

• Historical records from pre-colonial India mention trained Vaidyas (female physicians), yet by the colonial period, Indian women had almost no access to professional healthcare.

• Maternal mortality rates remained high due to this neglect, an issue still persistent in rural India today.

3. Economic Disenfranchisement of Women

Women in ancient India actively participated in trade, agriculture, and even governance. Queens like Ahilyabai Holkar ran successful economies, and inscriptions from ancient guilds mention female merchants and artisans. Yet, over time, historical biases eroded women's economic independence.

Causes of Decline:

• Misuse of Religious Texts: Selective interpretations discouraged women from working outside the home.

• Colonial Economic Policies: British taxation and land ownership laws prioritized men, displacing women from traditional professions

• Industrialization's Gender Bias: As modern industries emerged, male labor was preferred, further excluding women from financial independence.

Proof and Modern Consequences:

• Records from ancient Indian trade guilds show female merchants (Sreshthinis), proving their past economic role.

• Today, the gender wage gap and lack of women in leadership positions reflect the centuries-long erosion of their economic rights.

4. Political Exclusion of Women

Vedic and early historic India saw women rulers, advisors, and diplomats. However, historical biases slowly erased their presence from political decision-making.

Causes of Decline:

• Foreign Invasions and Political Instability: As invasions increased, political roles for women diminished for "protection" reasons.

• Colonial Suppression: British rule erased many indigenous governance structures where women had power.

• Social Norms Reinforcing Male Leadership: Even after independence, politics remained a male-dominated sphere.

Proof and Modern Consequences:

• The Arthashastra and inscriptions from Mauryan and Gupta times mention women in governance, contradicting modern misconceptions of their historical absence.

• Today, female political representation in India remains disproportionately low, despite constitutional reservations.

5. The Misrepresentation of Sati: A Colonial and Social Distortion

One of the most misrepresented aspects of Indian history is the practice of Sati, often portrayed as an inherent Hindu tradition when, in reality, it was never a prescribed religious practice in Hinduism. The colonial narrative—primarily pushed by British administrators and reformers—framed Sati as a barbaric custom deeply embedded in Indian society, justifying their so-called civilizing mission. However, historical evidence suggests that Sati was neither widespread nor mandated by Hindu scriptures. Instead, it was a phenomenon that arose due to social, political, and external pressures rather than religious doctrine.

Sati in Hindu Texts: What Do the Scriptures Say?

Hindu scriptures, especially the Vedas and Upanishads, do not prescribe Sati as a religious obligation. Instead, several texts explicitly discourage it:

 • Rigveda (10.18.8) initially describes a widow symbolically lying beside her deceased husband but then instructing her to rise and continue life, which is the opposite of Sati.

 • The Atharvaveda and Manusmriti emphasize widow remarriage, not self-immolation.

 • The Narada Smriti and Yajnavalkya Smriti refer to widows leading a dignified life of devotion and learning, not self-sacrifice.

 • In the Mahabharata, Kunti, the mother of the Pandavas, does not commit Sati despite being a devoted wife of Pandu. Similarly, Draupadi, who outlives her husbands, does not perform Sati.

If Sati was a religious obligation, these revered figures would have followed it. The fact that they did not proves that the practice was never a fundamental Hindu custom.

The Role of Foreign Invasions in the Spread of Sati

Sati became more prevalent after repeated foreign invasions, particularly during the medieval period when Muslim invaders targeted Hindu women. Mass rapes, forced conversions, and slavery of women were widespread under certain Islamic rulers, as recorded by chroniclers like Al-Biruni and Ibn Battuta. Fearing dishonor, some women resorted to Jauhar (mass self-immolation) as a desperate measure. Over time, this wartime strategy was confused with Sati, leading to its institutionalization in some regions.

This was not an organic Hindu practice but a reaction to extreme oppression. Many Rajput queens, for instance, committed Jauhar not due to religious belief but to escape brutality at the hands of invaders.

The British, however, failed to distinguish between Jauhar and Sati, further distorting history.

British Propaganda and Selective Abolition

The British made Sati one of their primary social reform causes, with figures like Raja Ram Mohan Roy championing its abolition. However, his credibility is disputed, as he worked closely with British officials, and his reformist stance conveniently aligned with the colonial narrative that justified British rule as a "civilizing mission."

Furthermore, while the British abolished Sati, they **conveniently ignored the horrific conditions they themselves imposed on Indian women**:

• British land revenue policies led to widespread poverty, increasing child marriages and forced prostitution.

• Indigo and tea plantations run by the British exploited Indian women as bonded laborers under inhumane conditions.

• Devadasi and temple prostitution systems were manipulated under British rule, with reports showing colonial officers taking advantage of these women.

This hypocrisy exposes how the British exaggerated certain social issues for their own benefit while ignoring their own atrocities.

The Truth About Sati

Sati was never a part of Hinduism but a social evil that arose due to war, political instability, and societal misinterpretations. It was neither widespread nor fundamental, and most Hindu texts emphasize widow remarriage, not self-immolation. The British, however, weaponized the image of the "burning Hindu widow" to justify their control over India while ignoring the oppression they themselves caused.Thus, any historical discussion of Sati must be grounded in facts, not colonial propaganda or selective narratives.

6. The Truth About Child Marriages

Ancient India allowed age-appropriate marriages, with scriptures mentioning Gandharva Vivaha (consensual marriages). However, historical biases led to child marriages.

Causes:

• Foreign Invasions: Many early child marriages were defensive strategies to protect girls from being abducted.

• Colonial Legalization: British-era laws recognized child marriage as a "custom" rather than eradicating it.

• Misinterpretation of Texts: Later religious justifications distorted original Vedic views on marriage age.

Proof and Modern Consequences:

• Manusmriti (9.94) advises marriage at a mature age, contradicting later child marriage practices.

• The Prohibition of Child Marriage Act (2006) is a modern correction of this historical bias.

My Opinion

Women in India have faced centuries of historical bias, often justified through misinterpretations of religious, social, and legal texts. However, the truth is clear: ancient Indian society valued women's contributions across multiple domains, and their decline was a consequence of external pressures and deliberate distortions.

The erasure of women's roles in education, health, economy, and politics was neither natural nor inevitable—it was engineered over centuries. Today, as historical research brings forward evidence contradicting these biases, it is crucial to acknowledge and correct the distortions.

Sati was never a Hindu practice but a tragic corruption. Child marriages were largely a survival mechanism during foreign invasions, not an inherent Indian tradition. The sooner we recognize these realities, the sooner we can break free from outdated biases and restore the dignity and rightful place of women in society.History has been unfair to women, but the present gives us a chance to set the record straight. The question is—**are we ready to do so**?

Chapter-8

Women in SouthIndia – Queens, Scholars, and Warriors

Women in South India: Queens, Scholars, and Warriors

History often remembers kings, but it is equally shaped by queens, warriors, scholars, and artists. The women of South India were never passive figures in history. From ruling vast kingdoms to influencing religion, literature, art, and trade, their impact is undeniable. Yet, their stories have often been overshadowed, forgotten, or misrepresented.

Through this chapter, I aim to uncover the remarkable contributions of South Indian women—leaders like Rani Rudrama Devi, scholars like Avvaiyar, and warriors like Velu Nachiyar—while also addressing the distortion of systems like the Devadasi tradition. These women shaped not just dynasties but entire civilizations, and their legacy is one that deserves to be retold.

The Queens Who Ruled

Rani Rudrama Devi (1259–1289 CE): The Warrior Queen of the Kakatiya Dynasty

In the 13th century, the Kakatiya kingdom of present-day Telangana witnessed something extraordinary—a woman ruling as a sovereign in a male-dominated world. Rani Rudrama Devi was not just a queen; she was a warrior who led her troops into battle, defending her empire from invasions.

To strengthen her claim to the throne, she was officially designated as a male ruler (Rajadhiraja), an unusual but necessary step to gain legitimacy in a time when female rulers were rare. She introduced strong administrative reforms and improved fortifications, ensuring that Warangal remained a major power.

Her reign saw economic stability, the promotion of trade, and the construction of temples.

Despite multiple threats from external invaders, including the Yadavas and the Pandyas, she held her ground. Even Marco Polo, the Venetian traveler, mentioned her in his accounts, describing her as a wise and capable ruler.

Rani Velu Nachiyar (1730–1796 CE): The First Indian Queen to Fight the British

Long before Rani Lakshmibai, another queen in South India took up arms against colonial rule. Rani Velu Nachiyar of Sivagangai (Tamil Nadu) was the first recorded queen to fight against the British East India Company. After her husband was killed in battle, she spent years planning her revenge, seeking alliances, and training an army that included women warriors (Udaiyal Padai).

In 1780, she executed a brilliant military strategy—using a human bomb, her loyal commander Kuyili, who set herself on fire to destroy British ammunition depots. Rani Velu Nachiyar successfully reclaimed her kingdom, proving that resistance against colonial forces began much earlier than mainstream history acknowledges.

Rani Mangammal (1689–1704 CE): The Diplomat Queen of Madurai

Rani Mangammal of the Nayak dynasty was known for her administrative skills, diplomatic prowess, and contributions to infrastructure. Unlike many queens who focused solely on military affairs, Mangammal expanded irrigation projects, built roads, and developed trade routes. She also played a crucial role in maintaining diplomatic relations with the Mughals and the Marathas, balancing regional politics with great skill.Her rule brought stability to Madurai, making it a significant political and economic center. She also encouraged the development of temples and religious institutions, strengthening cultural traditions in South India.

Women's Role in Temple Administration and Spiritual Traditions

Temple administration in South India was not solely in the hands of kings or Brahmin priests—women played a crucial role as well. Queens like Rani Mangammal and Ahilyabai Holkar contributed to temple construction and renovation. Women from various communities managed temple affairs, ensured the smooth conduct of religious rituals, and even made donations.

Women Saints and Philosophers

South India produced several female saints and philosophers who challenged norms and contributed to religious discourse.

• Andal (8th century CE) – A Tamil poet-saint of the Bhakti movement, Andal composed the Tiruppavai, devotional hymns dedicated to Lord Vishnu. She is revered as one of the twelve Alvars and remains a symbol of female devotion in Tamil Nadu.

• Akkamahadevi (12th century CE) – A mystic poet and devotee of Lord Shiva, Akkamahadevi defied social conventions, choosing a life of spiritual asceticism. Her vachanas (devotional poems) are among the finest works of Kannada literature.

• Avvaiyar (Various Periods) – The name "Avvaiyar" refers to multiple poetesses in Tamil history, known for their wisdom and literary works. Their compositions, including moral teachings and philosophical thoughts, influenced Tamil society for generations.

Women's Economic Contributions: Trade and Agriculture

Contrary to the notion that women were confined to domestic roles, historical records show that South Indian women played an active role in economic development.

• Guilds and Trade Networks – In medieval South India, women participated in trade, especially in textile production, jewelry making, and spice trade. Tamil inscriptions mention women merchants engaged in commerce across the Indian Ocean.

• Agriculture and Land Ownership – In certain dynasties, royal women owned agricultural lands and ensured fair distribution of resources. The Chola period saw women managing estates and supervising irrigation projects.

The Devadasi System: Its Sacred Origins and Later Distortion

The Devadasi system was once a revered institution in Hindu society, especially in South India. The word Devadasi translates to "Servant of God" (Deva = God, Dasi = female servant), reflecting the spiritual and cultural significance of these women. In its original form, the Devadasi system was not about oppression or exploitation but about devotion, art, and service to the divine.

Historically, Devadasis were dedicated to temple deities through a ritual known as Pottukattu (a symbolic marriage to the deity), after which they were considered lifelong servants of the temple. Their duties included maintaining temple traditions, performing sacred dances (Bharatanatyam, Odissi, etc.), singing devotional hymns, and participating in religious ceremonies.

They were well-versed in classical music, dance, and Sanskrit scriptures. Many Devadasis were highly educated, with knowledge of literature and philosophy. Unlike ordinary women in medieval society, they had financial independence and could own property.

Devadasis and Their Role in Society

• Custodians of Classical Arts — The temple dancers played a crucial role in preserving and passing down Bharatanatyam, Odissi, and Carnatic music. Some of the greatest compositions in Indian classical music were composed by Devadasis and their patrons.

• Religious and Social Influence — Devadasis held high status in society. They were respected figures who interacted with priests, scholars, and even royalty. Many temples had dedicated quarters (Agraharams) for them, where they lived and continued their service.

• Political Influence — In some periods, particularly under the Cholas and Vijayanagara rulers, Devadasis wielded significant influence in court affairs, acting as cultural ambassadors and temple administrators. Some Devadasis even became advisors to kings and queens.

For centuries, this tradition thrived. The presence of Devadasis was considered essential for temple rituals, as their dance and music were viewed as offerings to the divine.

The Decline: How Colonial Policies and Social Changes Corrupted the System

Despite its once-sacred status, the Devadasi system underwent a tragic transformation over time. Several factors contributed to its decline:

British Colonial Disruptions and Misrepresentation

• The British colonial administration did not understand the role of Devadasis in Hindu temples and classified them as mere "dancing girls".

• The British system of land revenue and taxation ended the traditional patronage that sustained Devadasis, pushing many into poverty.

• Christian missionaries, viewing the tradition through a Western moral lens, labeled the practice as immoral and began campaigns to "rescue" Devadasis.

• The Anti-Nautch Movement (1892) led by British-influenced social reformers equated temple dances with immorality, leading to widespread bans on Devadasi practices.

2. Economic Hardships and Social Stigma

• As temples lost royal patronage, Devadasis were left without financial support, forcing many to seek alternative livelihoods.

• Society, influenced by colonial narratives, began stigmatizing Devadasis as courtesans, though originally, they had been respected figures.

• Some unscrupulous elements in society exploited the economic vulnerability of Devadasis, distorting the tradition into something unrecognizable from its original form.

3. Laws Against the Tradition Without Understanding Its History

• The Madras Devadasis (Prevention of Dedication) Act, 1947 criminalized the dedication of women to temples. While it was meant to prevent exploitation, it also completely erased the role of Devadasis as cultural and artistic custodians.

- Many Devadasis, once respected for their art, were left without protection or dignity, as society now viewed them as outcasts.

The Need for Re-evaluation: Correcting the Narrative

While it is true that certain elements of the system became exploitative over time, it is equally important to recognize that the original Devadasi tradition was an integral part of temple culture and artistic heritage.

- The suppression of this system also led to the near extinction of temple dances like Bharatanatyam, which had to be revived later by artists like Rukmini Devi Arundale.

- Many inscriptions and temple records show that Devadasis were landowners, donors to temple construction, and patrons of literature—contrary to the colonial portrayal of them as oppressed women.

- Even today, many ancient temple sculptures depict Devadasis with pride, showcasing their vital role in spiritual life.

A Forgotten Legacy:

The Devadasi system, in its original form, was not about exploitation but about art, devotion, and social empowerment. However, due to colonial misrepresentation, economic decline, and later distortions, it transformed into a practice that lost its original sanctity.

Understanding the history of Devadasis is crucial because it reminds us that not all traditions are inherently oppressive—some have been distorted over time due to external influences and changing social structures.

Rather than outright condemnation, what is needed is a historical re-evaluation, one that separates the sacred past from the corrupted later practices, ensuring that the legacy of these remarkable women is not forgotten.

Conclusion:

The history of South Indian women is not just a tale of oppression—it is a story of power, resilience, and wisdom. These queens, scholars, and warriors were not passive participants in history but active architects of their times.

While later historical biases often tried to diminish their contributions, the evidence speaks for itself. Whether through governance, spirituality, trade, or the arts, South Indian women shaped the civilization we see today. Their impact, though at times forgotten, remains undeniable.

By reclaiming these stories, we do more than honor the past—we correct the narrative, ensuring that future generations recognize the true strength of the women who built, defended, and enriched South India.

CHAPTER-9
Concepts from Medieval India-
That
Redefined Gender Roles.

Concepts from Medieval India That Redefined Gender Roles

History is not just a record of battles and empires; it is also the story of how societies defined and redefined themselves. Among the many aspects of life that evolved over centuries, gender roles remain one of the most contested and often misunderstood subjects. Medieval India, a period marked by the rise and fall of powerful dynasties, was also a time of profound shifts in the perception of gender. Women were not merely passive figures in the background; they actively shaped the political, social, and economic landscapes of their time.

Yet, much of this history has been lost or distorted. Colonial narratives and foreign interpretations—particularly those influenced by Islamic and later British rule—sought to portray Indian women as oppressed and powerless. But the truth is far more complex. Women across different cultures and religions wielded authority, led armies, composed literature, and redefined societal norms. Some of these figures emerged as rulers, others as saints, warriors, and reformers. The stories of these women—and the broader gender dynamics of medieval India—deserve to be revisited without the biases imposed by external forces.

Women Who Defied Male Supremacy: Queens Who Ruled in Their Own Right

Medieval India saw a number of powerful queens who did not merely serve as consorts but actively governed and shaped the course of history. In an era where male-dominated rule was considered the norm, these women stood out as exceptional figures who defied the expectations of their time.

One such example is **Razia Sultana**, the only female ruler of the Delhi Sultanate. Her father, Sultan Iltutmish, saw in her a competent leader, surpassing her brothers in both intellect and capability. However, the idea of a woman on the throne was unacceptable to the Turkic nobility. Razia did not simply rule from behind the veil—she abandoned traditional feminine attire, dressed in male garments, and led her armies into battle. She was an administrator who introduced policies of meritocracy and religious tolerance, yet her reign was short-lived, as the male nobles conspired against her. Her downfall was not due to incompetence but because she had challenged the established gender hierarchy of Islamic rule in India.

Similarly, in the Mughal court, **Nur Jahan** became the de facto ruler of the empire during the reign of her husband, Emperor Jahangir. Unlike other queens confined to the palace, Nur Jahan issued official decrees in her own name, controlled trade, and even commanded the imperial army. Her authority, however, made her a target for resentment among the male-dominated Mughal nobility, and after Jahangir's death, her influence was systematically erased from official records.

Meanwhile, in South India, **Rani Rudrama Devi** of the Kakatiya dynasty ruled as a king rather than a queen. To reinforce her legitimacy, she adopted the male title "Maharaja" and led her troops personally into battle. Her rule saw significant architectural and economic advancements, yet later historians often overlooked her contributions.

Another formidable leader was **Velu Nachiyar**, the first Indian queen to fight against British colonial rule. Years before the famed Rani Lakshmibai, Velu Nachiyar waged war against the British East India Company, forming alliances with diverse communities, including both Hindu and Muslim warriors. Her courage and military strategy were unparalleled, but her story remains relatively unknown outside Tamil historical accounts.

These women were not anomalies; they were part of a larger tradition of female leadership that existed in India before patriarchal forces and colonial distortions sought to diminish their impact.

The Bhakti Movement and the Revolt Against Gender Norms

While women rulers fought on the battlefield, another movement was reshaping gender norms in a different way—the Bhakti movement. This spiritual uprising, which rejected rigid Brahmanical orthodoxy, provided women with a platform to challenge societal constraints.

Figures like Meerabai and Akka Mahadevi defied both familial and societal expectations. Meerabai, a Rajput princess, abandoned her royal life to become a wandering devotee of Krishna, composing poetry that critiqued patriarchal restrictions. Akka Mahadevi went even further—she renounced clothing altogether, symbolizing her rejection of worldly attachments and male-imposed modesty norms.

The Bhakti movement offered women an alternative space where devotion was prioritized over gender roles. However, colonial narratives later misinterpreted these women as mere victims of oppression rather than active participants in reshaping Indian society.

Dowry, Sati, and Child Marriage: Myths, Misinterpretations, and Historical Realities

Medieval India was a period of profound social transformation, influenced by foreign invasions, changing legal systems, and economic shifts. Among the most debated and misrepresented practices in Indian history are dowry, Sati, and child marriage—each of which evolved over centuries, often for reasons that had little to do with their later exploitative forms. Today, they are widely condemned as symbols of patriarchy, yet their origins tell a far more complex story.

The Truth About Dowry: A System Distorted by Time and Law

Dowry, in its present form, is seen as a social evil where a bride's family is burdened with giving large sums of money and gifts to the groom's family. However, this is a drastic corruption of what was originally a form of economic empowerment for women.

Dowry vs. Stridhan: Understanding the Difference

In ancient India, what is now called "dowry" was actually **Stridhan**, a system meant to provide financial independence to a woman within her marriage. The concept was designed so that a woman had personal wealth—land, gold, jewelry, and sometimes livestock—that could not be touched by her husband or in-laws.

• The Manusmriti (3.52) and Narada Smriti explicitly stated that Stridhan was a woman's exclusive property.

• Even the Arthashastra recorded that this wealth was meant to be a safeguard against mistreatment or abandonment.

So how did this change? The shift came during the medieval period, particularly under Islamic rule.

Medieval Changes: Dowry as Compensation for Lost Inheritance Rights

Islamic legal traditions, which governed large parts of India under the Delhi Sultanate and Mughal Empire, followed a different system of inheritance. In Hindu law, daughters could inherit family wealth, but Islamic law reduced women's inheritance rights, granting them only half of what male heirs received. This created an imbalance—Hindu families, especially those in regions under Muslim rule, began offering larger dowries to ensure their daughters' security in marriage.

By the time of British rule, dowry had transformed further. The British legal system codified Hindu personal laws but failed to recognize the concept of Stridhan, reducing women's financial autonomy even further. Instead of wealth given to women for their protection, dowry became a financial transaction between families, creating the exploitative system seen today.

Thus, dowry was never meant to oppress women. It became a burden only after foreign rule changed property rights and legal structures.

Sati: A Defensive Practice Turned into a Misunderstood Symbol

Few practices in Indian history have been as misunderstood and misrepresented as Sati—the self-immolation of widows. While colonial narratives painted it as a widespread Hindu custom, historical evidence suggests that it was never a mainstream practice and had specific socio-political roots.

The Vedic Perspective on Widows

Contrary to popular belief, Vedic texts did not support Sati. In fact, the Rig Veda (10.18.7) explicitly states that widows should return to society and remarry:

"Rise, woman, and come back to life. You have lived with your husband and made a home. Now go and live again among the living and bear children."

Similarly, the **Arthashastra** and **Dharmashastras** encouraged widow remarriage, proving that the idea of burning widows was not part of early Hinduism.

The Origin of Sati: A Wartime Sacrifice, Not a Religious Requirement

So where did Sati come from? The practice can be traced back to foreign invasions, especially from the 11th century onward when India faced brutal attacks from Islamic armies.

• Hindu women, especially Rajput queens, faced the horrific reality of being captured, raped, and enslaved by invading forces.

• In response, Jauhar—mass self-immolation—emerged as a desperate act of defiance, ensuring that women would not fall into enemy hands.

Notable instances of Jauhar include:

• The 1303 siege of Chittorgarh, where the women of the Rajput court burned themselves alive rather than be taken by Alauddin Khilji's army.

• The 1568 Jauhar of Rani Karnavati, when Akbar's forces attacked Mewar.

Over time, this extreme measure—originally practiced only in warrior communities during wartime—became ritualized in certain regions. However, it was never a pan-Indian practice, nor was it mandated by Hindu scriptures.

British Exploitation of Sati

The British outlawed Sati in 1829, portraying themselves as saviors of Indian women. However, they exaggerated its prevalence to justify colonial intervention, despite the fact that it was already declining.

Ironically, they ignored the widespread practice of widow-burning in Europe—especially in Ireland and parts of Russia—as well as the mistreatment of widows in Victorian England. This selective outrage highlights the political motivations behind the British campaign against Sati rather than genuine concern for women's welfare.

Child Marriage: A Social Defense Against Foreign Rule

Child marriage is often presented as an ancient Hindu custom, but historical records suggest that it was not a widespread practice before the medieval period.

Vedic Traditions and Marriageable Age

Ancient Indian texts provide clear guidelines for the ideal age of marriage:

• The Manusmriti (9.94-9.95) recommended 16 years for girls (SOME SCRIPTS SAY 18 YEARS)and 25 years for boys—far older than the child marriages seen in later periods.

• The Mahabharata and Ramayana depict heroines like Draupadi and Sita, who married at an appropriate age, indicating that childhood marriage was not the norm.

Why Did Child Marriage Increase?

The real rise of child marriage can be traced back to foreign invasions and socio-political instability:

1. Islamic rule brought mass enslavement and forced conversions. Young Hindu girls were kidnapped, forcibly married to Muslim rulers, and sold in markets from Afghanistan to the Middle East.

2. To protect daughters from abduction, Hindu families married them off early, ensuring that they were legally bound to a husband before invaders could claim them.

3. In regions controlled by the Mughals and later British, the abolition of women's property rights meant that an unmarried girl was seen as economically vulnerable.

Thus, child marriage was not a religious tradition but a desperate response to centuries of foreign domination.

British Double Standards on Child Marriage

Ironically, while the British condemned child marriage in India, they allowed it within their own empire. Victorian England had no minimum marriage age, and girls as young as 12 were married off in aristocratic families. In fact, legal reforms against child marriage in India came much later than in Europe.

Conclusion: Reclaiming the Truth About Indian Traditions

The misrepresentation of dowry, Sati, and child marriage has been one of the greatest distortions of Indian history. What began as systems of women's financial security, wartime resistance, and social protection were later manipulated by foreign laws, invasions, and colonial propaganda.

• Dowry was originally Stridhan, meant to give women financial independence. It turned into a burden only after Islamic inheritance laws and British legal changes stripped women of their property rights.

• Sati was never a Hindu religious practice but a desperate wartime sacrifice in the face of foreign invasions.

• Child marriage was not an ancient Hindu tradition but a defensive strategy against the mass abductions of Hindu women by foreign invaders.

The rewriting of Indian history—first by Islamic rulers, then by British colonizers—has shaped modern perceptions, leading many to falsely believe that these were Hindu traditions from time immemorial. It is time to correct these misconceptions and recognize that Indian society has always had the ability to evolve, adapt, and reform its traditions when freed from external distortions.

CHAPTER-10
Daughters of Dharam

The Storm of Invasions: A Civilization in Turmoil

The land of Bharat had long been a cradle of civilization, where women held positions of reverence as scholars, warriors, and spiritual guides. However, the course of history was violently disrupted when foreign invasions swept across the Indian subcontinent, bringing with them not just the clash of swords but the imposition of alien customs that sought to suppress the autonomy of its people—particularly its women.

With the arrival of the Arab, Turkic, and Mughal invaders, Indian society was forced into a period of resistance, not just against military conquest but against an ideological war that threatened to erase its cultural ethos. Women became the first and most brutal victims of this war. The once-revered daughters of dharma, who had debated in royal courts and ridden into battlefields, were now hunted, enslaved, and forced into silence. Yet, their spirit was not extinguished.

This chapter explores the horrors faced by Indian women during foreign invasions, their indomitable survival, and the ways in which they resisted the attempts to erase their dignity and existence.

The Shadow of Slavery: Indian Women as the First Targets

The Arab and Turkic invasions of India were not merely military conquests; they were also campaigns of forced conversions, mass enslavement, and brutal exploitation. The invaders followed the traditions of war that allowed the capture and enslavement of women as war booty, a practice widely recorded in their own chronicles.

From **Mohammad bin Qasim's** conquest of Sindh in 712 CE to Mahmud of Ghazni's repeated raids in the 11th century, the pattern remained the same—after the armies had vanquished local rulers, the women were taken as spoils of war. Al-Utbi, a chronicler of Mahmud of Ghazni, proudly recorded how thousands of Hindu women were captured and sent to the slave markets of Ghazni and Baghdad, where they were sold like commodities.

Even more disturbing was the fate of Rajput women during the later Delhi Sultanate and Mughal rule. The most infamous of these accounts is the sack of Chittorgarh in 1303 CE by Alauddin Khilji. When faced with certain defeat, Rani Padmini and thousands of Rajput women committed Jauhar—self-immolation—to avoid being taken as slaves. The flames that engulfed these women were not just a desperate act of escape but a statement of defiance against an enemy that sought to strip them of their dignity.

Such horrors were not limited to one kingdom or region. During Timur's invasion of India in 1398, Delhi's women were systematically abducted and sold into slavery. Babur's own memoirs, the Baburnama, boast about the women taken as prisoners of war. This brutal legacy continued throughout the Mughal era, especially during the reign of Aurangzeb, when women of captured Hindu and Sikh families were forcibly converted or sent to harems.

But history does not record only the suffering; it also records the fierce resistance.

The Sword and the Veil: Women Who Fought Back

Not all women accepted their fate passively. Across India, queens, warrior women, and commoners alike took up arms, devised strategies, and ensured that their voices were not silenced.

Rani Karnavati and the Rajput Spirit

Rani Karnavati of Mewar, upon realizing that Bahadur Shah of Gujarat was marching towards her kingdom, did not wait for her fate to be sealed. She sent the legendary rakhi to Humayun, a symbolic request for help, showcasing a woman's ability to command alliances even in times of crisis. Though Humayun arrived late, Karnavati's resolve became a beacon of inspiration.

Chand Bibi: The Warrior of Ahmednagar

Chand Bibi, a queen of Ahmednagar, was one of the few women rulers who directly fought the Mughal forces. Unlike many others who were forced into subjugation, she led her army from the front, personally strategizing defenses against Akbar's expansionist ambitions.

Velu Nachiyar: The Lioness of Tamil Nadu

Down south, Velu Nachiyar, long before the great rebellion of 1857, waged war against the British, proving that resistance was not limited to North India. She formed alliances, trained her own women's army, and launched an attack on British forces, reclaiming her territory.

While some fought with swords, others fought by preserving their traditions, refusing to bow to oppressive customs, and ensuring that their daughters were raised with the same indomitable spirit.

The Suppression of Voices: Erasing Women from History

One of the most tragic consequences of these foreign invasions was the systematic erasure of women from historical records. While Hindu, Jain, and Buddhist traditions had celebrated female scholars, rulers, and warriors, the Islamic and colonial rulers ensured that women were reduced to footnotes.

Education, which had once been accessible to both men and women in ancient India, was denied to women under Islamic rule. Temples, which served as centers of learning, were destroyed, cutting off women's access to knowledge. In regions under the Mughal rule, harems became prisons, locking away royal women and ensuring that their political influence was curbed.

Later, the British colonialists further distorted Indian history, painting a picture of Indian women as eternally oppressed, thereby justifying their own rule as a "civilizing mission." In reality, Indian women had been resisting oppression for centuries—against foreign invaders, against imposed traditions, and against every force that sought to suppress them.

A Consequence of Foreign Invasions

One of the biggest misinterpretations of Indian history has been the practice of Sati and child marriage, both of which were not a part of Vedic Hinduism but rather defensive reactions to foreign rule.

Sati: The Truth Behind the Fire

Contrary to colonial propaganda, Sati was never a Hindu religious obligation. The Rig Veda (10.18.7) clearly states that widows should remarry, not self-immolate. The practice of Jauhar, often mistaken for Sati, emerged during Islamic invasions as a way for

Rajput women to avoid being captured and taken to harems. The British, however, exaggerated its prevalence to justify their interference in Indian customs.

Child Marriages: A Survival Mechanism

Child marriages, too, were a result of foreign invasions. Before the advent of Islamic rule, Hindu texts prescribed marriage at a mature age. The Manusmriti (9.94-9.95) suggests an ideal marriageable age of 16 for girls and 25 for boys. However, with the constant threat of abductors during the Sultanate and Mughal periods, families began marrying their daughters off early to protect them.

Yet, these practices, which were meant to be temporary defenses, were later distorted and institutionalized, further restricting women's freedoms.

Conclusion: The Unbreakable Spirit of Indian Women

Despite centuries of oppression, Indian women never surrendered. From the warrior queens who rode into battle to the silent resistance of mothers who preserved their traditions in the face of oppression, women ensured that the essence of Indian civilization remained intact.The daughters of dharma have always been warriors, even when they held no swords. They have fought against invaders, against unjust traditions, and against every force that sought to suppress them. Their stories must be told, not just as history but as inspiration.

India's women were never passive victims—they were, and always will be, the unbreakable backbone of this civilization.

CHAPTER-11
Colonial Shadows– Women under British Rule

Colonial Shadows: Women Under British Rule

The arrival of the British in India was not merely the imposition of a foreign administration; it was the beginning of an era that fundamentally altered the social, economic, and political landscape for Indian women. Unlike the Mughal or pre-Islamic Indian periods, where women—despite challenges—had access to power, education, and even military roles, British rule systematically stripped them of these opportunities. Colonial rule did not just exploit India's wealth; it reshaped Indian society in a way that deepened gender inequalities, often under the guise of "civilizing" the natives.

This chapter explores the colonial impact on women across various sectors, revealing how British policies led to economic disempowerment, legal subjugation, and social marginalization of Indian women.

1. The Economic Disempowerment of Women

Before British rule, women actively participated in local economies, often as traders, artisans, weavers, and agricultural laborers. The traditional Indian economy had guilds where women had roles, and many families engaged in cottage industries. However, British economic policies devastated these indigenous industries, forcing women into poverty.

With the introduction of British-manufactured goods, Indian handloom industries collapsed. Women who were skilled in spinning and weaving—such as those in Bengal's muslin industry—lost their livelihood overnight. Many families that once depended on female artisans now faced financial ruin. The destruction was so severe that British officials themselves admitted that India's self-sufficient economy was crumbling under their policies. William Bentinck, Governor-General of India, noted that the muslin weavers of Dhaka were "starving" as British imports replaced native textiles.

Furthermore, the Permanent Settlement Act of 1793, which introduced zamindari land reforms, deprived many rural women of their rights to land inheritance and agricultural work. Previously, women from peasant and tribal communities had roles in farming and land management, but British legal frameworks only recognized male ownership, making women increasingly dependent on male relatives for survival.

2. The Impact on Women's Education

Contrary to colonial narratives, pre-British India had a tradition of female scholars, teachers, and poets. Women like Gargi and Maitreyi in ancient India, and later Bhakti poet-saints like Mirabai and Akka Mahadevi, were intellectual figures who shaped religious and social discourse. However, under British rule, women's education was largely ignored.

While the British introduced Western-style education, their schools were primarily designed for elite men. Missionary schools for women were rare and focused more on Christian conversion than real empowerment. Even the so-called reforms in education often catered only to upper-class women, leaving the majority of Indian women—especially in villages—without access to learning.

A British official, James Mill, in his History of British India, famously dismissed Indian education as primitive, conveniently ignoring the fact that even in pre-colonial times, certain Hindu and Jain communities had centers of female education. The colonial education system did not uplift Indian women; rather, it created a new class divide where a small number of elite women received British-style education while the majority remained deprived.

3. Legal Subjugation: How British Laws Restricted Women's Rights

One of the most damaging aspects of British rule was the introduction of colonial laws that reinforced patriarchal control over women. Before British rule, many Hindu and Islamic legal traditions had provisions for women's property rights, widow remarriage, and female inheritance. The British, however, implemented a rigid legal system that institutionalized women's subordination.

The introduction of the Anglo-Hindu Law and Anglo-Mohammedan Law distorted indigenous legal traditions. For instance:

• Hindu women traditionally had the right to inherit ancestral property under certain conditions. However, the British codification of Hindu law in the 19th century heavily favored male heirs.

• Widow remarriage, which was allowed in many Indian communities, became increasingly stigmatized under British rule as Victorian morality influenced Indian society.

• Women in Islamic communities who previously had financial independence through Meher (a mandatory payment to wives in Islamic marriages) found their rights undermined by British modifications to Sharia law.

British policies did not just fail to improve women's rights; they made them worse. By enforcing a European legal framework that ignored India's diverse cultural traditions, British rule placed women in a more vulnerable position than before.

4. The Physical and Social Abuse of Women Under British Rule

One of the darkest aspects of British colonialism was the physical and social abuse Indian women suffered at the hands of British officers and soldiers. Reports from the time reveal shocking incidents of sexual violence, particularly during the Revolt of 1857, when British troops retaliated against Indian civilians with horrific brutality.Women in Kanpur, Delhi, and Lucknow were subjected to systematic assaults during the British reprisals after the mutiny. The rape and abuse of Indian women by British soldiers were often ignored by colonial authorities, and few perpetrators were punished. British officials, under the guise of "restoring order," frequently targeted women from families suspected of supporting the rebellion.

Moreover, the British introduced systems of legal prostitution in India, particularly in cantonment areas, where poor Indian women were forced into sexual slavery to serve British soldiers. The Contagious Diseases Act of 1864 institutionalized this practice by subjecting Indian women to medical inspections while leaving British men unaccountable.While some British historians later romanticized their rule as a period of reform, the reality is that British officers often exploited Indian women under the pretext of "protecting" them from oppressive native customs.

5. British Distortion of Indian Social Practices

The British justified their rule by portraying Indian society as backward and oppressive to women. While it is true that some harmful practices like sati and child marriage existed, the British exaggerated their prevalence and used them as an excuse for intervention.

For example, sati was never a widespread Hindu practice. Historical records suggest that it was largely confined to certain Rajput communities and became more common only during Islamic invasions as an act of self-immolation to avoid enslavement. The British, however, sensationalized it, claiming that all Hindu widows were forced into the practice, which was far from the truth.

Similarly, child marriage, while existing in some parts of India, was often a defensive strategy against foreign invasions rather than a core Hindu tradition. The British overlooked the fact that child marriages were still practiced in Victorian England, instead choosing to vilify Indian culture while ignoring similar problems in their own society.

Colonial Shadows: Women Under British Rule

The Great Bengal Famine: A Manufactured Catastrophe

The Great Bengal Famine of 1943 was not a natural disaster—it was a crime. A deliberate policy of exploitation, food hoarding, and wartime profiteering orchestrated by British officials turned the fertile lands of Bengal into a graveyard. Over three million people perished, and among them, it was the women who suffered in the worst ways imaginable.

Starvation did not discriminate between class or caste. Mothers, too weak to move, watched their children die before them. Young girls, their bodies reduced to mere skeletons, were sold into prostitution just to earn a handful of rice. In Calcutta, British soldiers and Indian elites took advantage of desperate women, offering food in exchange for their dignity. There were stories of women lining the streets, waiting outside military barracks in the hope of receiving leftover scraps—some never returned.

Winston Churchill, the man often glorified as a war hero, dismissed their suffering with cold indifference. When informed of the mass starvation, he simply remarked, "If food is so scarce, why hasn't Gandhi died yet?" The British Empire did not just rob India of its wealth; it robbed its women of their last shred of humanity.

Women and the World Wars: The Forgotten Victims

While Britain fought wars across Europe, it drained India of its resources, forcing men into battle and leaving women behind to pick up the pieces of shattered households. Over two million Indian soldiers were sent to fight in World War I, and in their absence, women took on the roles of farmers, laborers, and caregivers—unrecognized and unpaid. The colonial government, however, saw them as nothing more than collateral damage.

During World War II, British military establishments in India became hubs of violence against women. British officers frequently abducted local women to serve as "comfort women" for their troops, similar to what the Japanese Imperial Army did in Korea. These women were never acknowledged, never compensated, and never given justice.

Meanwhile, Indian women working in British-controlled factories and war industries were subjected to inhumane conditions. They worked long hours, inhaled toxic fumes, and suffered from malnutrition, all while being paid far less than their British counterparts. If they protested, they were beaten or fired.

Even within their own families, Indian women faced a new struggle—the loss of their men. Husbands, fathers, and brothers were conscripted into the war effort, often never to return. Widows of fallen soldiers were not given pensions, and in their desperation, many were forced into destitution. The war did not bring them honor or recognition; it only brought more suffering.

The Weight of Forgotten Wounds

History often remembers the victors, the rulers, and the battles fought on grand stages. But beneath the surface of India's colonial past lies a deeper, more painful story—the suffering of its women, whose lives were altered in ways history barely acknowledges. British rule did not merely exploit the nation's resources; it dismantled the social and economic fabric that once upheld women's dignity and agency.

For centuries, Indian women held positions of power, shaped religious traditions, and contributed to intellectual and economic life. Under colonial rule, they were stripped of these roles, reduced to objects of exploitation, silenced under unjust laws, and forgotten in the larger political narrative. They faced violence, displacement, and erasure, yet their struggles were dismissed as collateral damage in the fight against imperialism.

But the question remains—has India itself ever truly acknowledged this? Did the post-independence governments ever make an effort to recognize the suffering of women under British rule? History textbooks speak of economic drain, political subjugation, and the exploitation of resources, but where are the stories of the women who bore the brunt of colonial oppression? Where is the justice for those who were trafficked, abused, and silenced?

Independence brought freedom from colonial rule, but it did not erase the scars. The British left, but the damage they inflicted—socially, economically, and psychologically—was never fully addressed. Even after independence, little was done to restore what was lost. The legal system, once designed to protect British officers from accountability, remained flawed. The social injustices that took root under colonial policies were allowed to fester. And the women who had suffered? They were left to pick up the pieces without recognition, without reparations, without even an acknowledgment of their pain.

A nation that forgets its wounded cannot truly heal. Until the full weight of this history is confronted—until the resilience of those women is honored, and their suffering acknowledged—not just by historians, but by the Indian state itself—true justice remains incomplete. The past cannot be rewritten, but it must be remembered. Only then can history move forward with truth, rather than silence.

CHAPTER-12
THE AWAKENING –
WOMEN IN FREEDOM STRUGGLE

The Awakening Woman in India's Freedom Struggle

History remembers the men who stood at the forefront of India's battle for independence, their names etched into textbooks and speeches. Yet, behind every revolution, behind every call for freedom, there were women—resilient, fearless, and relentless in their pursuit of justice. Some have received their due recognition, but many remain hidden in the shadows of history, their sacrifices overlooked, their voices unheard.

These women did not merely participate; they shaped the very course of India's independence movement. They were warriors, spies, strategists, and orators. They suffered imprisonment, bore the brunt of colonial cruelty, and yet, they persevered. Their contribution was not just regional but part of a collective national struggle.

The Torchbearers of Revolution: Women from Different Regions

India's freedom movement was not fought on a single battlefield, nor was it the effort of a single leader. It was a nationwide resistance, with every region producing its own revolutionaries.

India's journey to independence is adorned with the sacrifices and valor of countless women, many of whom remain lesser-known or forgotten. Their unwavering commitment and diverse roles were instrumental in shaping the nation's destiny. Here are some of these remarkable women:

1. Ammu Swaminathan (1894-1978):

Born in Palghat, Kerala, Ammu Swaminathan was a prominent freedom fighter and social activist. She was an active participant in the Indian independence movement and later became a member of the Constituent  Assembly, contributing to the framing of the Indian Constitution. Her dedication to social causes continued post-independence, focusing on women's rights and education.

2. Dakshayani Velayudhan (1912-1978):

Hailing from Kerala, Dakshayani Velayudhan was the first and only Dalit woman to be elected to the Constituent Assembly of India. She played a crucial role in advocating for the rights of the marginalized and was instrumental in shaping policies related to social justice in the nascent stages of the Indian republic.

3. Hansa Jivraj Mehta (1897-1995):

A reformist, social activist, and writer from Gujarat, Hansaben Mehta was a prominent figure in the freedom struggle. She was a member of the Constituent Assembly and played a significant role in drafting the Indian Constitution. Her efforts extended to championing women's rights and education, leaving a lasting impact on Indian society.

4. Kamla Chaudhary (1908-1970):

Born in Uttar Pradesh, Kamla Chaudhary was an active participant in the freedom movement and a member of the Constituent Assembly. She contributed to various social causes, including women's empowerment and education, and played a role in shaping the policies of independent India.

5. Leela Roy (1900-1970):

A fierce freedom fighter from Assam, Leela Roy was known for her revolutionary activities and close association with Netaji Subhas Chandra Bose. She was a member of the Constituent Assembly and worked tirelessly for women's education and social reforms, leaving an indelible mark on the nation's progress.

6. Malati Choudhury (1904-1998):

Hailing from Odisha, Malati Choudhury was a devoted Gandhian and freedom fighter. She participated in the Salt Satyagraha and was imprisoned for her involvement in the Quit India Movement. Post-independence, she continued her work in social reform, focusing on rural development and education.

7. Purnima Banerjee (1911-1951):

From Uttar Pradesh, Purnima Banerjee was an active participant in the freedom struggle and a member of the Constituent Assembly. She was known for her dedication to social causes, including women's rights and education, and played

a significant role in shaping the policies of independent India.

8. Rajkumari Amrit Kaur (1889-1964):

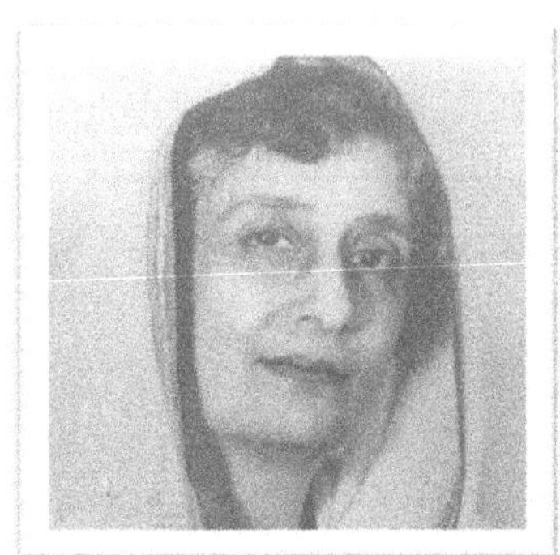

Born into the royal family of Kapurthala, Rajkumari Amrit Kaur was a staunch freedom fighter and social reformer. She served as the first Health Minister of independent India and was instrumental in establishing the All India Institute of Medical Sciences (AIIMS). Her contributions to public health and women's rights have left a lasting legacy.

9. Renuka Ray (1904-1997):

A prominent freedom fighter and social activist from West Bengal, Renuka Ray was a member of the Constituent Assembly and played a significant role in shaping India's social policies. She was a strong advocate for women's rights and worked tirelessly towards social welfare and reform.

10. Sucheta Kriplani (1908-1974):

Born in Ambala, Sucheta Kriplani was a freedom fighter and politician. She played a crucial role during the Quit India Movement and later became the first woman Chief Minister of Uttar Pradesh. Her dedication to public service and nation-building remains exemplary.

11. Vijayalakshmi Pandit (1900-1990):

Sister of Jawaharlal Nehru, Vijayalakshmi Pandit was an influential freedom fighter and diplomat. She was the first woman to hold a cabinet position in pre-independent India and later became the first female President of the United Nations General Assembly.

12. Annie Mascarene (1902-1963):

Hailing from Kerala, Annie Mascarene was a freedom fighter and politician. She was one of the first women to be elected to the Indian Parliament and played a significant role in the integration of princely states into the Indian Union. Her political acumen and dedication to the nation were instrumental during the formative years of independent India.

13. Bishni Devi Shah (1902-1972):

An unsung hero from Uttarakhand, Bishni Devi Shah was the first woman from the region to be jailed during India's independence movement. She actively participated in protests, encouraged the use of Khadi, and supported the families of imprisoned freedom fighters. Her relentless dedication to the cause of freedom exemplifies the spirit of countless unnamed women who contributed to India's independence.

14. Aruna Asaf Ali (1909-1996):

Known as the 'Grand Old Lady of the Independence Movement,' Aruna Asaf Ali played a crucial role in the Quit India Movement. She is renowned for hoisting the Indian National Congress flag at the Gowalia Tank Maidan in Mumbai in 1942, signaling the commencement of the movement. Despite facing imprisonment and going underground to evade arrest, her resolve remained unshaken. Post-independence, she continued to work for social welfare and was awarded the Bharat Ratna in 1997.

15. Bhikaji Cama (1861-1936):

A prominent figure in the Indian independence movement, Bhikaji Cama was a staunch advocate for women's rights and equality. She is best remembered for unfurling the first version of the Indian national flag at the International Socialist Conference in Stuttgart, Germany, in 1907, garnering international attention for India's plight under British rule. Her efforts in mobilizing support for India's freedom on foreign soil were instrumental in the global awareness of the cause.

16. Durgawati Devi (1907-1999):

An active participant in revolutionary activities, Durgawati Devi, also known as 'Durga Bhabhi,' was closely associated with Bhagat Singh and Chandrashekhar Azad. She played a pivotal role in aiding Bhagat Singh's escape after the Saunders' assassination by disguising herself as his wife. Her courage and commitment made her a significant yet unsung heroine of the freedom struggle.

17. Kamaladevi Chattopadhyay (1903-1988):

A multifaceted personality, Kamaladevi Chattopadhyay was not only a freedom fighter but also a social reformer and an advocate for the arts. She was the first woman to run for a legislative seat in India and played a significant role in the Salt Satyagraha of 1930. Post-independence, she was instrumental in reviving Indian handicrafts and handlooms, contributing immensely to the cultural renaissance of the nation.

18. Tara Rani Srivastava (1919-2008):

Hailing from Bihar, Tara Rani Srivastava was an active participant in the Quit India Movement. Alongside her husband, she led a procession to hoist the Indian flag at the Siwan police station. Despite her husband being fatally shot during the protest, she continued to lead the march and attempted to hoist the flag, exemplifying unparalleled bravery and dedication to the cause of freedom.

19. Moolmati :

The mother of the revolutionary Ram Prasad Bismil,Moolmati's contribution to the freedom struggle is often overlooked. Her unwavering support and resilience, especially during her son's imprisonment and subsequent execution, reflect the silent yet profound sacrifices  made by countless mothers during the independence movement.

20. Padmaja Naidu (1900-1975):

Daughter of Sarojini Naidu, Padmaja Naidu was actively involved in the freedom struggle from a young age. She was imprisoned for her participation in the Quit India Movement and later served as the Governor of West Bengal. Her dedication to public service extended to her role as the longest-serving president of the Indian Red Cross Society. 

21. Snehlata Varma (1911-2013):

A freedom fighter from Uttar Pradesh, Snehlata Varma participated in various movements against British colonial rule. She was imprisoned multiple times for her involvement in protests and was known for her efforts in mobilizing women to join the freedom struggle.

22. Umabai Kundapur (1892-1992):

A dedicated activist from Karnataka, Umabai Kundapur was instrumental in organizing women volunteers during the freedom movement. She managed the 'Bhagini Mandal,' a women's volunteer corps, and worked closely with prominent leaders to promote Khadi and Swadeshi goods, emphasizing self-reliance and national pride.

23. Bina Das (1911-1986):

A revolutionary from Bengal, Bina Das is known for her daring attempt to assassinate the British Governor of Bengal, Stanley Jackson, in 1932. Though the attempt was unsuccessful, her fearless act at the age of 21 highlighted the intense desire for independence among the youth. She endured rigorous imprisonment but remained steadfast in her commitment to the nation's freedom.

24. Kittur Rani Chennamma (1778-1829):

The queen of the princely state of Kittur in Karnataka, Rani Chennamma led an armed rebellion against the British East India Company in 1824, predating the 1857 revolt. Despite her capture and imprisonment, she remains a symbol of resistance against colonial rule.

25. Lakshmi Sahgal (1914-2012):

A revolutionary and officer of the Indian National Army (INA), Captain Lakshmi Sahgal was a close associate of Netaji Subhas Chandra Bose. She led the Rani of Jhansi Regiment, the women's unit of the INA, and later continued her service as a physician and social activist.

26. Matangini Hazra (1870-1942):

An active participant in the Quit India Movement, Matangini Hazra was affectionately known as "Gandhi Buri" (Old Lady Gandhi). At the age of 72, she led a procession in Tamluk, West

Bengal, and was fatally shot by British police while holding the Indian flag.

27. Kanaklata Barua (1924-1942):

A young freedom fighter from Assam, Kanaklata Barua joined the Quit India Movement. At 17, she led a procession to hoist the national flag at a local police station and was shot dead by British forces, becoming a martyr for the cause.

28. Bhogeswari Phukanani (1885-1942):

An Assamese freedom fighter, Bhogeswari Phukanani played a significant role in the Quit India Movement. She was killed while leading a protest against British authorities, symbolizing the courage of women in India's liberation struggle.

29. Rani Gaidinliu (1915-1993):

A Naga spiritual and political leader, Rani Gaidinliu led a revolt against British rule in Manipur and Nagaland. Arrested at 16, she spent 14 years in prison and was released after independence, continuing to work for the upliftment of her people.

30. Usha Mehta (1920-2000):

Known for organizing the Congress Radio, an underground radio station, during the Quit India Movement, Usha Mehta disseminated news and messages to keep the spirit of resistance alive. Her efforts were crucial in maintaining morale during the struggle.

31. Durgabai Deshmukh (1909-1981):

A freedom fighter and social reformer, Durgabai Deshmukh participated in the Salt Satyagraha and was imprisoned for her activities. Post-independence, she was a member of the Constituent Assembly and worked tirelessly for women's rights and education.

32. Kamala Nehru (1899-1936):

Wife of Jawaharlal Nehru, Kamala Nehru was an active participant in the Non-Cooperation Movement. She organized protests, led picketing of foreign goods, and worked relentlessly to involve women in the freedom struggle.

33. Sarala Devi Chaudhurani (1872-1945):

A prominent figure in Bengal's freedom movement, Sarala Devi was instrumental in promoting Swadeshi and nationalist ideals. She founded the first women's organization in India, Bharat Stree Mahamandal, aiming to promote education and self-reliance among women.

34. Libia Lobo Sardesai (born 1924):

A freedom fighter from Goa, Libia Lobo Sardesai, along with her husband Vaman Sardesai, operated an underground radio station called "Voice of Freedom" from 1955 to 1961. This station broadcasted messages advocating for Goa's liberation from Portuguese rule. Following Goa's independence, she became the first Director of Tourism for Goa, Daman, and Diu. In recognition of her contributions, she was honored with the Padma Shri in 2025.

35. Tara Rani Srivastava:

An ardent participant in Mahatma Gandhi's Quit India Movement, Tara Rani Srivastava, along with her husband Phulendu Babu, led a procession aiming to hoist the Indian flag at the Siwan police station in Bihar. During the protest, her husband was fatally shot, but Tara Rani continued to lead the march and attempted to hoist the flag, exemplifying unparalleled bravery and dedication to the cause of freedom.

Women Freedom Fighters of Hyderabad State: The Struggle Against the Nizam and British

Hyderabad State, ruled by the Nizam, was one of the last princely states to be integrated into India. The struggle here was twofold—against British imperialism and the oppressive rule of the Nizam, who resisted joining independent India. Women in Hyderabad played a significant role in both the anti-colonial movement and the fight against the feudal system that denied them basic rights.

1. Suravaram Pratapa Reddy's Women Activists

While Suravaram Pratapa Reddy is known for his literary and nationalist contributions, several women activists from Hyderabad followed his ideology and worked to raise awareness about self-rule. Women from middle-class backgrounds took up roles in the Andhra Mahila Sabha, a key organization promoting education and political awareness.

2. Rani Rudrama Devi (Pre-British Era, but a Symbol of Resistance)

Although she ruled much before the British arrived, Rani Rudrama Devi of the Kakatiya dynasty (present-day Telangana) became an icon of female leadership. Her legacy inspired later generations of women to take part in political struggles.

3. Bhagya Reddy Varma's Movement and Dalit Women Fighters

Bhagya Reddy Varma led a social reform movement in Hyderabad, and his efforts encouraged Dalit women to break social barriers and fight for their rights. Women from his movement became vocal participants in protests against both the British and the feudal landlords under the Nizam.

4. Sarojini Naidu (Hyderabad-born, National Leader)

While Sarojini Naidu is often associated with national politics, she was born in Hyderabad and became the "Nightingale of India." She actively participated in the Non-Cooperation Movement, Civil Disobedience Movement, and Quit India Movement, becoming one of the few women to be arrested multiple times by the British.

5. Jamalunnisa Begum – The Revolutionary Against the Nizam

Jamalunnisa Begum was one of the fiercest women who opposed both British rule and the Nizam's refusal to join India. She was associated with the Hyderabad State Congress and led women's marches against the feudal system, advocating for the integration of Hyderabad with India.

6. Komaram Bheem's Women Warriors

While Komaram Bheem led the Gond tribal resistance against the Nizam, several tribal women fought alongside him. These unsung heroines took part in armed struggles, resisting the Nizam's oppressive tax policies and forced labor systems.

7. The Women of the Telangana Rebellion (1946-1951)

One of the largest peasant uprisings in India, the Telangana Rebellion saw thousands of women joining armed struggles against the feudal landlords (doras) and the Razakars, the Nizam's private militia.

- **Mallu Swarajyam** – A fearless guerrilla fighter who joined the Communist-led Telangana Rebellion against the Nizam's oppressive rule. She led several attacks on feudal landlords who exploited peasants.

- **Chityala Ailamma** (Chakali Ilamma) – A Dalit woman who defied a landlord's attempt to seize her land. She became a symbol of the peasant uprising and inspired thousands of women to take up arms.

- **Jaunty Bheemabai** – Another key figure in the Telangana struggle, she was part of the underground resistance against both the British and the Nizam's forces.

8. Women Who Defied the Razakars

The Razakars, a paramilitary force supporting the Nizam, committed atrocities against those demanding Hyderabad's integration into India. Women like Rama Bai, Savitri Bai, and Nagamma played crucial roles in underground resistance movements, hiding activists, smuggling weapons, and providing intelligence to Indian nationalist groups.

The Collective Strength: Hyderabad's Women in India's Freedom Struggle

The women of Hyderabad did not just fight against colonial rule; they stood against a deeply entrenched feudal system, religious extremism, and social inequality. They bore the brunt of violence but continued their resistance. Their struggle was not just about national freedom but about social justice and human dignity.

Conclusion: The Unacknowledged Pillars of Freedom

As the pages of history unfold, they often carry the weight of injustice—not because they lack stories, but because they fail to tell them all. India's fight for independence was not just a tale of a few celebrated names; it was a collective struggle, a movement powered by countless men and women who dared to dream of a free nation. Yet, while history books have ensured that some names are never forgotten, far too many remain in the shadows, their sacrifices overlooked, their legacies lost in the passage of time.

The women of India's freedom struggle were more than just participants; they were strategists, warriors, revolutionaries, and torchbearers of resistance. They stood shoulder to shoulder with their male counterparts, often bearing greater burdens—fighting not just colonial oppression but also deep-rooted societal constraints. Some took up arms, leading battles that shook the British Empire, while others waged silent wars, smuggling intelligence, nursing wounded revolutionaries, and sustaining the movement from within their homes. Their fight was not just for independence but for justice, for dignity, and for the right to stand as equals in a new India.

Yet, despite their undeniable contributions, how many of their names do we truly remember? How often do we speak of the fearless revolutionaries like Pritilata Waddedar, Bina Das, and Durgawati Devi with the same reverence as their male counterparts? How many of these women find a place in school textbooks, on statues, or in public memory? The answer is unsettling. While a few names—Rani Lakshmibai, Sarojini Naidu, Kasturba Gandhi—have been rightfully honored, thousands of others remain forgotten, their sacrifices acknowledged only in passing or not at all.

And what has the Indian government done to rectify this? Has there ever been a sincere effort to recognize and commemorate these countless women who laid down their lives for the nation? Have they been given their due place in national narratives, or do they remain confined to rare mentions in academic discussions? Even decades after independence, their recognition remains insufficient, their stories lost beneath layers of neglect.

It is impossible to name every single woman who fought for India's freedom, for they are countless. Many remain unknown, unrecorded, and unsung, their contributions buried with them. To those whose names history has forgotten, to those who never received their due honour, to those whose   sacrifices paved the path to independence but were never acknowledged—we owe an apology.

But apologies are not enough. Remembrance is a duty. Their courage, their sacrifices, and their unwavering resolve must not be remembered merely as footnotes in history but as integral chapters in India's story. These women were not just witnesses to change; they were its architects. India did not gain independence on the shoulders of men alone—it was the relentless spirit of both men and women that led the nation to freedom.

It is time we recognize them all.

CHAPTER-13
NEW DAWN
OF
EMPOWERMENT

Women's empowerment in India has undergone a profound transformation over the years. From the struggles of the pre-independence era to the post-independence legal reforms and the modern socio-economic revolution, women have fought to secure their rightful place in society. This chapter explores the evolution of women's rights movements, the leaders who championed their cause, landmark legal judgments, and the changing landscape of gender roles. However, it also emphasizes the responsible use of legal protections, ensuring that laws meant to uplift women are not misused against men, as true empowerment is rooted in justice and fairness.

The Rise of Women's Rights Movements: Pre- and Post-Independence

Pre-Independence: Women as the Pillars of Resistance

The foundations of women's empowerment were laid during India's freedom struggle. Women actively participated in protests, underground resistance, and revolutionary activities. Sarojini Naidu, Kamala Nehru, Aruna Asaf Ali, Captain Lakshmi Sahgal, and Usha Mehta were some of the key figures who fought alongside men for independence.

Organizations like the All India Women's Conference (AIWC) and Bharat Stree Mahamandal provided platforms to demand education and equal rights. These movements shaped the consciousness of Indian women, proving that they were not just homemakers but also warriors of change.

Post-Independence: The Constitutional Guarantee of Equality :

After independence, the Indian Constitution laid the foundation for gender equality. Under the guidance of Dr. B.R. Ambedkar, several key provisions were included to ensure women's rights:

- Right to Vote (1950) – Unlike many Western nations, Indian women had voting rights from the very beginning.

- Article 14 (Right to Equality) – Ensured no discrimination based on gender.

- Article 15(3) – Allowed the state to make special provisions for women and children.

- Article 39(d) – Promoted equal pay for equal work.

Despite these constitutional guarantees, gender disparity persisted. Women's rights movements in the 1970s and 1980s focused on labor rights, domestic violence, and reproductive rights. The 1990s and 2000s saw debates on workplace equality, marital rights, and financial independence, further strengthening women's empowerment.

Feminist Leaders and Landmark Legal Reforms

Feminist Leaders Who Reshaped India

Several women have played an instrumental role in India's feminist movement:

- Ela Bhatt – Founder of SEWA, empowering self-employed women.

- Aruna Roy – Fought for labor rights and transparency in governance.

- Medha Patkar – Led the Narmada Bachao Andolan, highlighting the displacement of women in rural areas.

- Kamaladevi Chattopadhyay – Worked for women's economic independence and handloom revival.

• Sudha Murthy – A champion for rural women's education and healthcare.

These leaders emphasized empowerment through education, financial independence, and legal awareness, rather than through the misuse of laws.

Landmark Legal Rulings: Empowerment vs. Misuse

Over the decades, legal reforms have been crucial in securing women's rights. However, with great power comes responsibility. It is important for women to use these laws for protection and justice, not for revenge or personal gain.

1. Right to Equal Inheritance – Vineeta Sharma v. Rakesh Sharma (2020)

This judgment ensured that daughters had equal rights in ancestral property, reinforcing financial independence.

Responsible Use – Women should claim what is rightfully theirs but avoid engaging in false property disputes that could damage family relations.

2. Decriminalization of Adultery – Joseph Shine v. Union of India (2018)

This ruling struck down Section 497 IPC, affirming that women were not the property of their husbands.

Responsible Use – While this law removed outdated gender biases, relationships should be built on trust rather than exploiting legal loopholes to justify unethical behavior.

3. Right to Enter Temples – Indian Young Lawyers Association v. State of Kerala (2018)

The Supreme Court ruled that women of all ages had the right to enter the Sabarimala temple, ensuring religious equality.

Responsible Use – Women should respect traditions while fighting for their rights, ensuring that reforms lead to social harmony rather than division.

4. Permanent Commission for Women in Armed Forces – Ministry of Defence v. Babita Puniya (2020)

This ruling allowed women to serve in commanding roles in the military.

Responsible Use – Women in defense forces should use their roles to inspire leadership rather than demand special privileges.

5. Triple Talaq Abolition – Shayara Bano v. Union of India (2017)

The Supreme Court declared instant triple talaq unconstitutional, protecting Muslim women from arbitrary divorce.

Responsible Use – Women should ensure their rights in marriage without using laws unfairly against their partners for personal gain.

6. The Dowry Prohibition Act (1961) & Section 498A IPC

Laws were created to protect women from harassment and domestic violence. However, there have been cases of misuse, where false cases were filed for revenge or monetary settlements.

Responsible Use – Women should use these laws as shields, not swords. False accusations harm genuine victims and weaken the credibility of legal protections.

The Changing Social and Economic Landscape for Women

Women in Education: A Pathway to True Empowerment

Education has been the cornerstone of women's empowerment in India. <u>Female literacy rates have crossed 70%,</u> with increasing participation in higher education. Initiatives like:

- **Beti Bachao, Beti Padhao** – Encouraging girls' education.

- **National Scheme for Incentive to Girl Child** – Financial aid for school-going girls.

- **Women in Science & Engineering (WISE) Initiative** – Promoting female participation in STEM.

The rise of educated women in law, business, technology, and medicine has challenged stereotypes and given women financial independence.

Women in Governance: Balancing Power with Responsibility

Political participation has increased, with women serving as MPs, MLAs, and Chief Ministers. The reservation of seats in Panchayati Raj institutions has empowered rural women.

True Empowerment – Leadership should not be about quotas but about competence. Women should earn their positions rather than demand them based on gender alone.

Women in Science and Technology: Breaking Barriers

Indian women have made remarkable contributions:

- Dr. Tessy Thomas – India's "Missile Woman."

- Dr. Gagandeep Kang – Leading vaccine researcher.

• Ritu Karidhal & Muthayya Vanitha – ISRO scientists behind Chandrayaan & Mangalyaan.

Empowerment is about ability, not privilege – Women should enter fields based on merit rather than expect opportunities solely based on gender.

Misuse of Women-Centric Laws: Notable Instances

1. Section 498A of the Indian Penal Code (IPC):

Designed to protect married women from cruelty by their husbands and in-laws, Section 498A has, in some cases, been exploited to harass innocent individuals. The Supreme Court, in Arnesh Kumar v. State of Bihar (2014), acknowledged the misuse of this provision and issued guidelines to prevent unnecessary arrests.

2. The Dowry Prohibition Act, 1961:

Intended to combat the dowry system, this act has sometimes been misused to file false cases against husbands and their families. Legal experts have highlighted the need for a filtration mechanism to curb the filing of such false cases.

3. The Protection of Women from Domestic Violence Act, 2005:

While this act aims to protect women from domestic abuse, there have been instances where it has been misused. The Supreme Court has warned against the misuse of this law, emphasizing that filing false cases can lead to legal consequences.

Legal Remedies for Those Falsely Accused

If an individual believes they have been falsely accused under these laws, several legal remedies are available:

1. Anticipatory Bail:

Given that offenses under Section 498A are non-bailable, obtaining anticipatory bail is crucial to prevent immediate arrest. A well-prepared application should highlight the false nature of

the allegations and the accused's willingness to cooperate with the investigation.

2. Filing a Counter-Case:

The accused can initiate legal proceedings against the complainant for defamation under Section 500 of the IPC or for providing false evidence under Section 340 of the Code of Criminal Procedure (CrPC).

3. Seeking Legal Redress:

Approaching higher courts to quash false charges is a viable option. The judiciary has, in several instances, quashed baseless FIRs to prevent misuse of the legal system.

4. Gathering Evidence:

Collecting evidence that disproves the allegations, such as communication records or witness testimonies, can strengthen the defense. Presenting such evidence can lead to the dismissal of false charges.

Measures for Courts to Address False Accusations

To ensure justice and prevent the misuse of women-centric laws, courts can adopt the following measures:

1. Scrutinizing Complaints:

Courts should meticulously examine the credibility of allegations, ensuring that frivolous or malicious complaints are identified early in the legal process.

2. Penalizing False Accusations:Imposing penalties on individuals who file false cases can serve as a deterrent against the misuse of protective laws.

3. Ensuring Fair Trials:

Guaranteeing that the accused receives a fair trial, with opportunities to present evidence and defend themselves, is paramount to upholding justice.

4. Implementing Guidelines for Arrests:

Adhering to established guidelines, such as those from the Arnesh Kumar case, can prevent unnecessary arrests and protect innocent individuals from undue harassment.

Below are notable examples illustrating such misuse:

1. Misuse of Dowry Laws:

- Atul Subhash Suicide Case (2024): Atul Subhash, a tech professional from Bengaluru, was found dead in his residence in December 2024. He left a suicide note alleging harassment by his wife and her relatives, accusing them of misusing dowry laws to extort money. He also mentioned alleged corruption involving a judge overseeing his case. This incident underscores concerns about the potential misuse of anti-dowry laws to harass or extort individuals.

2. Misuse of Sexual Harassment Laws:

• Jasleen Kaur Harassment Controversy (2015): Jasleen Kaur accused Sarvjeet Singh of sexual harassment in Delhi, leading to his arrest and widespread media condemnation. However, an eyewitness later supported Singh's innocence, and in 2019, he was acquitted of all charges. This case highlights how false allegations can severely impact the lives of the accused.

3. Misuse of SC/ST (Prevention of Atrocities) Act:

• Vishnu Tiwari Case: Vishnu Tiwari was falsely implicated in a rape case under the SC/ST Act and spent 20 years in prison before being acquitted by the Allahabad High Court in 2021. This case highlights concerns about the misuse of protective laws leading to wrongful incarceration.

Addressing False Accusations:

To prevent the misuse of protective laws and ensure justice for all, the following measures can be considered:

• **Thorough Investigation**: Law enforcement agencies should conduct meticulous investigations before making arrests to ensure that allegations are credible.

• **Legal Safeguards**: Courts should implement guidelines to prevent misuse of laws, such as those established in the Arnesh Kumar v. State of Bihar case, which aimed to prevent unnecessary arrests under Section 498A of the IPC.

• **Penalizing False Accusations**: Individuals found guilty of filing false complaints should face legal consequences to deter the misuse of protective laws.

- **Public Awareness:** Educating the public about the serious implications of filing false allegations can promote responsible use of legal provisions.

Conclusion: The New Dawn of Empowerment – A Legacy to Uphold

Empowerment is not merely about rights, laws, or policies—it is about the soul of a civilization, the spirit of its people, and the sacrifices made to shape a just society. Women today stand on the shoulders of countless individuals—known and unknown, men and women alike—who have fought, bled, and even perished to carve a future where equality is not a privilege but a birthright.

When we speak of empowerment, we must not forget the fathers who toiled day and night to educate their daughters, the brothers who stood as silent shields against injustice, and the sons who grew up believing in the dignity and strength of women. Empowerment is not a war between genders but a shared responsibility—one that recognizes both sacrifice and support.

History has seen men lay down their lives to protect women from foreign invasions, from oppression, from the horrors of war and displacement. During the Bengal famine, men perished in hunger to feed their wives and daughters. During colonial rule, husbands and sons fought against tyranny, often knowing they might never return, just so their mothers and sisters could live in a free nation. Even in modern times, countless men have silently played their part—supporting women in their aspirations, standing beside them as equals, and fighting for their rights in courts and streets alike.

But true empowerment is not just about recognizing the past; it is about shaping the future responsibly. Rights must not be weapons but tools of justice. The misuse of laws meant for protection only weakens the cause of genuine victims and breeds resentment where there should be solidarity. A truly empowered woman is not one who misuses power but one who embodies wisdom, resilience, and fairness.

As the sun rises on this new dawn of empowerment, let us not divide ourselves into men and women, but stand together as human beings—upholding justice, ensuring dignity, and never forgetting the countless sacrifices that have made this moment possible. A better world is not built through conflict, but through understanding, gratitude, and shared progress.

This is not just the dawn of women's empowerment—this is the dawn of a more just, balanced, and awakened society.

CHAPTER-14
BREAKING BARRIERS –
WOMEN IN ACTION

Breaking Barriers: Women in Action

A woman's journey is often filled with unspoken sacrifices, silent struggles, and untold triumphs. For centuries, she was told where she belonged, what she could dream, and how far she could go. But today, in every corner of India, women are reshaping those boundaries—not with protests or defiance alone, but with sheer brilliance, resilience, and action.

This chapter is not about the battles they fought in the past—it is about the victories they are winning today, the milestones they are achieving, and the dreams they are turning into reality. It is about women who are not just breaking barriers but setting new horizons—in science, technology, space, medicine, defense, governance, and policy-making.

As you read their stories, remember—these are not just names in history books. These are daughters, sisters, mothers, and leaders who carry the weight of a billion dreams on their shoulders and still stand tall.

Women in STEM: The Power of Intelligence and Innovation

In the grand laboratories of ISRO, in the cutting-edge biotech firms, in the artificial intelligence labs of India's top universities—women are leading scientific revolutions.

When Tessy Thomas was a child, she would watch missiles being tested near her home in Kerala. Years later, she did not just watch them—she built them. Today, she is known as "India's Missile Woman", leading the development of the Agni-IV and Agni-V missiles. In a field where women were once invisible, she is untouchable in excellence.

Dr. Gagandeep Kang, the woman who gave India its first indigenous rotavirus vaccine, did not just create a medicine—she saved millions of children from a deadly virus.

And then there is Muthayya Vanitha, the first woman to lead an ISRO mission. When India's Chandrayaan-2 mission was about to launch, it was her decisions that guided the team. With every launch, these women are proving that space belongs not just to men in suits but to women in saris and lab coats alike.

Women in Medicine: The Healing Hands of a Nation

For centuries, women were told that their hands belonged in the kitchen. Today, their hands are saving lives.

In 1986, Dr. Indira Hinduja delivered India's first test-tube baby, bringing hope to countless couples who thought they would never hold a child of their own.

Dr. Padmavati Iyer, India's first female cardiologist, broke into a male-dominated field and built an empire of heart care in India. Dr. Soumya Swaminathan, the former Chief Scientist of WHO, played a crucial role in controlling tuberculosis—one of the deadliest diseases in India.

These women do not just heal patients. They heal the very system that once tried to keep them out.

Women in Defense: The Daughters Who Guard India

For decades, women were told they were too delicate to serve on the frontlines. Today, they are flying fighter jets, leading naval missions, and commanding battalions.

Flight Lieutenant Avani Chaturvedi became India's first female fighter pilot, soaring through the skies in a MiG-21 Bison, proving that bravery knows no gender.

Lieutenant General Punita Arora, the highest-ranking woman in the Indian Army, did not just break a glass ceiling—she marched through it in uniform.

And in 2023, **Shivangi Singh** became India's first woman Rafale pilot, maneuvering one of the world's most advanced fighter jets with grace, precision, and power.

Every time these women put on their uniforms, they carry the weight of history—and the dreams of every girl who ever wanted to protect her motherland.

Women in Civil Services: The Architects of Change

Politics and governance were once considered the business of men. But today, India's policies, reforms, and justice systems are shaped by women of wisdom, courage, and intellect.

• Kiran Bedi, the first woman IPS officer, cleaned up Tihar Jail and redefined police reforms.

• Smita Sabharwal, known as the People's Officer, transformed public administration with innovative governance.

• Upma Chawdhry, the first female director of LBSNAA, training future IAS officers to lead with vision and integrity.

These women do not just enforce laws; they shape the future of India.

Women in Policy and Economics: Driving India's Growth

In the halls of Parliament and in the offices of India's largest financial institutions, women are making decisions that impact 1.4 billion lives.

• **Nirmala Sitharaman**, India's first full-time female Finance Minister, is leading the nation's economic policies, proving that financial strategy is not a man's domain.

• Women-led startups in AI, biotech, and renewable energy are now some of India's fastest-growing enterprises.

Every policy they design, every budget they draft, every reform they implement—it is not just for the present but for generations of women who will follow.

Recent Milestones: The Future is Now • ISRO's Chandrayaan-3 and Aditya-L1 missions had record participation from women scientists.

• India's first all-women naval crew, who sailed across the world, proved that the sea does not care for gender—it only respects skill.

• Women-led defense startups are now supplying cutting-edge technology to the armed forces.

• The Supreme Court ruling on NDA recruitment for women opened new doors for military leadership.

Every step forward is not just an achievement—it is a statement.

A Message to Every Woman Reading This

You have heard that women are strong. But let me tell you what strength truly is.

Strength is Tessy Thomas, watching missiles as a child and dreaming of building them.

Strength is Dr. Gagandeep Kang, saving a million children without ever holding them.

Strength is Avani Chaturvedi, breaking the sound barrier in a MiG-21.

Strength is Kiran Bedi, walking into a prison and turning criminals into reformed men.

Strength is you.

This is your era. Not because someone gave it to you, but because you took it.

You are not waiting for a place at the table. You are building the table, writing the rules, and leading the conversation.

To the fathers and brothers who support their daughters and sisters, to the men who stand beside them—not as protectors, but as equals—this is your fight too.

And to the women reading this, remember: You are not just part of India's progress. You are the very force driving it forward.

The barriers are not just breaking anymore—they are disappearing.

The future is not waiting for you. It is yours to create.

CHAPTER-15
The Political and Social Reformers

Throughout India's history, women have been at the forefront of political and social reforms, challenging norms and pioneering changes that have profoundly influenced the nation's trajectory. This chapter delves into the remarkable contributions of women in politics, social reform, and movements that have redefined modern India.

Indira Gandhi: The Iron Lady of India

Indira Gandhi stands as a towering figure in Indian politics, serving as the country's first and, to date, only female Prime Minister. Her tenure, spanning from 1966 to 1977 and then from 1980 until her assassination in 1984, was marked by significant events that shaped India's political landscape. Gandhi's leadership during the Indo-Pakistani War of 1971 led to the creation of Bangladesh, showcasing her decisive and bold decision-making skills.

Her policies, including the Green Revolution, transformed India's agricultural sector, aiming for self-sufficiency in food production. However, her tenure also faced criticism, notably during the Emergency period (1975-1977), when civil liberties were suspended, the press was muzzled, and opposition leaders were imprisoned. Her era remains one of the most controversial in India's democratic history—celebrated for her leadership yet criticized for authoritarian tendencies.

Sarojini Naidu: The Nightingale of India

Sarojini Naidu was not only a prolific poet but also a freedom fighter and a significant political figure. She became the first woman governor in independent India, overseeing the United Provinces (now Uttar Pradesh). Naidu's eloquence and passion made her a prominent figure in the Indian National Congress, where she advocated for civil rights, women's emancipation, and anti-imperialistic ideas.

She played a crucial role in India's struggle for independence and was an inspiration for future generations of women in leadership. Her efforts to elevate women's participation in politics were groundbreaking in an era when female political representation was minimal.

Sucheta Kriplani: A Trailblazer in Governance

Sucheta Kriplani etched her name in history by becoming India's first female Chief Minister, leading the state of Uttar Pradesh from 1963 to 1967. Her tenure was marked by efforts to improve labor laws, strengthen governance, and enhance state infrastructure.

As an active participant in the Quit India Movement, she was deeply committed to India's independence and later dedicated herself to public service. Her leadership in handling labor unrest and economic challenges proved that women were equally capable of governing complex political landscapes.

Contemporary Women Leaders: Progress and Criticism

Women continue to make significant strides in Indian politics, but their tenures have not been free from scrutiny.

• Sonia Gandhi emerged as a pivotal figure in the Indian National Congress, leading the party through various electoral battles. However, her Italian origin has remained a subject of controversy, with critics questioning whether a foreign-born leader should have such a significant influence on India's governance. Despite this, she played a crucial role in forming coalition governments and supporting progressive welfare policies.

• Mamata Banerjee, the founder of the All India Trinamool Congress, became the first female Chief Minister of West Bengal. Her policies on social welfare, rural development, and women's safety have earned her widespread support. However, her tenure has not been without controversy—she has faced backlash for allegedly failing to act decisively in high-profile crimes, such as the doctor rape case, leading to criticism from both opposition leaders and activists.

• Nirmala Sitharaman broke barriers by becoming India's first full-time female Finance Minister, overseeing significant economic policies, defense budgets, and financial reforms. While her tenure has been praised for bold economic decisions, including corporate tax cuts and pandemic relief measures, she has also faced criticism for handling inflation and employment crises.

These leaders reflect both progress and challenges—showcasing the growing role of women in Indian politics while also highlighting the expectations and scrutiny that female leaders face.

Trailblazing Social Reformers: Champions of Equality and Education

Savitribai Phule: Pioneer of Women's Education

Savitribai Phule, along with her husband Jyotirao Phule, was a trailblazer in promoting women's education in 19th-century India. In 1848, she established the first school for girls in Pune, challenging the prevailing caste and gender biases of the time.

Her relentless efforts laid the foundation for the women's rights movement in India, emphasizing that education was the key to breaking social and economic oppression. Despite facing harassment and societal resistance, she remained steadfast in her mission to empower women and lower-caste communities.

Kanak Mukherjee: Advocate for Women's Rights

Kanak Mukherjee was instrumental in founding the National Federation of Indian Women (NFIW) in 1954, an organization affiliated with the Communist Party of India. The NFIW focused on women's labor rights, social injustices, and political representation.

Mukherjee's activism played a crucial role in mobilizing women from marginalized sections, advocating for equal pay, maternity benefits, and protection against workplace exploitation. Her work remains a foundation for modern labour laws concerning women.

The Women's Movement of the 1970s and 1980s

The late 20th century witnessed a resurgence of women's activism in India. The Mathura rape case in 1972, where a young tribal girl was raped by policemen, sparked nationwide protests, leading to significant reforms in India's rape laws.

This period marked a shift from localized struggles to a more organized women's movement, addressing issues such as domestic violence, workplace harassment, and political representation.

Contemporary Movements and Their Influence

In recent years, women-led movements have continued to shape India's socio-political fabric:

- Anti-Corruption Protests – Women played pivotal roles in the anti-corruption movements, demanding transparency and accountability in governance.

• Environmental Activism – Female activists have led campaigns against deforestation, climate change, and industrial pollution, advocating for sustainable development.

• Social Media Campaigns – The rise of digital platforms has allowed women to spearhead online campaigns addressing sexual harassment (#MeTooIndia), body shaming, mental health awareness, and workplace discrimination, leading to broader societal discussions and policy changes.

Community Media Initiatives: Voices from the Grassroots

Grassroots initiatives like Sangham Radio, India's first all-female community radio station run by Dalit women in Telangana, have empowered rural communities by addressing local issues, providing health tips, and preserving cultural narratives.

Such platforms have become instrumental in giving a voice to marginalized sections, fostering grassroots democracy and social change.

Conclusion

The contributions of women in India's political and social spheres have been monumental. From pioneering education reforms to leading the nation, their relentless pursuit of equality and justice has left a lasting imprint on modern India. However, leadership is never without its complexities—while some have been hailed for their vision and resilience, others have faced criticism for their decisions and governance. Yet, even those who have faced scrutiny have shaped India's trajectory in significant ways, for better or worse.

As India continues its journey toward progress, it is evident that women in power have played a crucial role, whether through policy changes that have benefited the masses or through leadership that has sparked both admiration and debate. Figures like Nirmala Sitharaman, who once faced criticism, have also earned recognition for reforms that directly impacted millions. This nuanced legacy reminds us that leadership is a dynamic force—one that is constantly judged, reassessed, and, ultimately, remembered for its influence on the people it serves.

CHAPTER-16
Women in Modern India – PEOPLE WHO ASPIRE

In the past, knowledge was confined to the privileged few, access to resources was determined by societal structures, and women were often left at the margins of technological and educational advancements. However, the modern Indian woman is no longer a silent observer—she is an active participant, shaping the world around her. The 21st century has witnessed an unprecedented transformation in the way women access knowledge, work, and lead, with technology playing the role of a great equalizer.

From a rural girl using a smartphone to educate herself beyond the limits of a traditional classroom to a young entrepreneur leveraging digital platforms to build a global business, technology has broken the barriers that once restricted women. The increasing access to mobile devices, internet connectivity, and digital learning platforms has opened a new world of opportunities, empowering women in ways unimaginable just a few decades ago.

Women and Technology: Shaping the Future

With the rapid growth of India's technology sector, women have stepped into roles that were once male-dominated. Today, women are not just users of technology but its creators, innovators, and leaders.

• Women in STEM (Science, Technology, Engineering, and Mathematics): The number of Indian women pursuing careers in STEM fields is steadily rising, thanks to initiatives like Digital India and Skill India. Women scientists have played a crucial role in major projects, including ISRO's Mars Orbiter Mission, which had a significant female workforce.

• Tech Entrepreneurship: Digital platforms have enabled women to start businesses from anywhere, overcoming traditional barriers of investment and infrastructure. Many women-led startups, such as Falguni Nayar's Nykaa and Richa Kar's Zivame, have revolutionized the Indian market.

• Coding and Artificial Intelligence: As AI and machine learning shape the future, Indian women are increasingly taking up roles in data science and software development, ensuring their voices are present in shaping the digital revolution.

The Socially Conscious Woman: Driving Change

Women have not only entered boardrooms and laboratories but have also become key players in social reforms and environmental activism. Unlike past generations, where activism was limited to physical protests and meetings, modern women are using digital tools to amplify their voices.

• Environmental Activism: Women like Vandana Shiva have led movements for sustainable agriculture, while young activists have taken to social media to raise awareness about climate change. Grassroots movements like the Chipko Movement, led by women, set the foundation for environmental activism, which continues today through initiatives focused on waste management, sustainable fashion, and conservation efforts.

• Sustainable Development Initiatives: Women entrepreneurs are actively leading the way in eco-friendly businesses, from sustainable fashion brands to zero-waste startups. Digital platforms have allowed these initiatives to reach a global audience, increasing awareness and impact.

• Women in Policy Making: From village-level leadership to international organizations, women are influencing policies that promote sustainability, gender equality, and social welfare.

Entrepreneurship: Women Building Empires

Economic independence is one of the strongest pillars of empowerment, and women in India are redefining success through entrepreneurship.

• Women-Led Startups: From beauty and fashion to finance and technology, Indian women are creating multi-million-dollar businesses. Women like Upasana Taku (co-founder of MobiKwik) and Suchi Mukherjee (founder of LimeRoad) are making their mark in the financial and e-commerce industries.

• Homegrown Businesses and Digital Marketplaces: Social media platforms like Instagram and Facebook have become launchpads for small-scale women entrepreneurs, enabling them to sell handmade crafts, organic products, and boutique services.

• Government Support for Women Entrepreneurs: Initiatives like the Stand-Up India Scheme provide financial assistance and mentorship to female business owners, helping them scale their ventures.

Government Schemes: Bridging the Gap

Recognizing the need for structured support, the Indian government has introduced various schemes that cater to women's education, employment, health, and financial independence.

• **Beti Bachao, Beti Padhao**: This initiative promotes education for girls, ensuring that more women gain access to higher education and career opportunities.

- **Ujjwala Yojana:** Aimed at rural women, this scheme provides LPG connections to households, reducing health hazards caused by traditional cooking fuels.

- **MUDRA Yojana**: This program offers financial support to women entrepreneurs, enabling them to start small businesses without the burden of high-interest loans.

- **Mahila E-Haat**: An online marketing platform for women entrepreneurs to showcase and sell their products globally.

- **Sukanya Samriddhi Yojana**: A savings scheme designed to provide financial security for young girls, encouraging long-term investment in their education and future.

Women Entrepreneurs: The Architects of Change

Falguni Nayar: The Self-Made Billionaire

Falguni Nayar, a former investment banker, changed the landscape of India's beauty and wellness industry with Nykaa, a company she founded in 2012. With a sharp business acumen and an unrelenting vision, she transformed Nykaa into a multi-billion-dollar empire, making her one of India's wealthiest self-made women. Under her leadership, Nykaa went public in 2021, cementing her status as a game-changer in India's entrepreneurial world.

Vineeta Singh: The Woman Who Redefined Beauty Standards

The co-founder of Sugar Cosmetics, Vineeta Singh, disrupted the beauty industry by creating a brand that resonated with Indian skin tones and preferences. A Shark Tank India investor, she is an advocate for women in business and continuously promotes financial independence for Indian women.

Kiran Mazumdar-Shaw: The Pioneer of Biotech in India

Kiran Mazumdar-Shaw's journey from being denied a job as a brewmaster to founding Biocon, one of India's largest pharmaceutical firms, is inspirational. Her company played a critical role in making affordable medicines accessible, proving that women can lead in science and industry.

Other Notable Entrepreneurs:

- **Ghazal Alagh (Mamaearth)** – Revolutionized the organic skincare industry.

- **Radhika Ghai Aggarwal (ShopClues)** – Created a digital marketplace for small businesses.

- **Suchi Mukherjee (Limeroad)** – Pioneered an innovative social commerce platform.

Women in Music: Voices That Resonate

Indian music has been enriched by phenomenal female singers who have not only entertained millions but have also redefined the industry.

Lata Mangeshkar: The Voice of India

Known as the Nightingale of India, Lata Mangeshkar's six-decade-long career made her a legend. With songs in multiple languages, she became the voice of generations, leaving behind an unmatched legacy.

S. Janaki: The Nightingale of the South

A legendary playback singer, S. Janaki's contributions to Telugu, Tamil, and Kannada music remain unparalleled. Her ability to bring out deep emotions in songs made her an irreplaceable icon.

Shreya Ghoshal: The Modern Melody Queen

With a voice that blends tradition with contemporary music, Shreya Ghoshal has dominated Bollywood and regional music alike. A winner of multiple National Awards, she is a symbol of consistency and grace in the industry.

Other Prominent Female Singers:

• **Chitra** – A versatile singer with numerous awards across South Indian languages.

• **Sunidhi Chauhan** – Known for her bold and powerful voice.

• **Geetha Madhuri** – A prominent Telugu playback singer.

Women in Dance: Masters of Grace and Rhythm

Indian classical and contemporary dance forms have thrived because of extraordinary female performers who have dedicated their lives to preserving and evolving the art.

Rukmini Devi Arundale: The Revivalist of Bharatanatyam

Rukmini Devi Arundale transformed Bharatanatyam from a temple art to a globally recognized dance form. She introduced theatrical elements and brought a spiritual touch to her performances, making her one of the most influential figures in Indian classical dance.

Mallika Sarabhai: The Dancer Who Fought for Social Justice

A renowned Bharatnatyam and Kuchipudi dancer, Mallika Sarabhai used dance as a medium to address social issues such as gender inequality and caste discrimination.

Madhuri Dixit: The Bollywood Diva Who Made Dance Popular

With her classical training and Bollywood presence, Madhuri Dixit redefined cinematic dance, making Kathak and semi-classical styles accessible to mainstream audiences.

Other Famous Dancers:

- **Shovana Narayan (Kathak)** – A legend in classical dance.

- **Yamini Krishnamurthy (Bharatanatyam & Kuchipudi)** – A Padma Vibhushan awardee.

- **Sudha Chandran** – Overcame disability to become a leading Bharatanatyam dancer.

The Rise of Women YouTubers: Digital Influence for Social Change

With digital platforms reshaping media consumption, several female YouTubers have emerged as powerful voices for social change.

Abhi and Niyu: The Duo That Educates India

While Abhi and Niyu work together, Niyu's perspective in their content is vital in making societal issues relatable. They focus on positive storytelling, educating people about India's unsung heroes, environmental conservation, and economic awareness. Despite criticism for their idealistic approach, they continue to influence millions with research-backed narratives that drive constructive discourse.

Prajakta Koli: The Voice of the Youth

Starting as a comedy content creator, Prajakta Koli (MostlySane) has expanded her influence into activism. She has collaborated with global initiatives such as the UN's Creators for Change program, focusing on gender equality and climate change.

Other Influential Female YouTubers:

- **Sejal Kumar** – Spreads awareness on mental health and body positivity.

- **Shweta Vijay Nair** – Promotes sustainable living and women's health.

- **Aditi Shrivastava (Menstrupedia)** – Uses digital media to educate people about menstrual health.

Conclusion: The Road Ahead

India stands at the cusp of a transformation where its women are no longer just participants but leaders in shaping the nation's future. From boardrooms to laboratories, from music studios to digital platforms, from the silver screen to the political arena—women today are not just finding spaces but are creating them. They are no longer waiting for opportunities; they are forging their own paths.

Yet, this journey has not been without struggle. For centuries, women have battled systemic oppression, societal expectations, and deeply ingrained biases. But every challenge has been met with resilience, every barrier with defiance. Today, as we witness women leading billion-dollar companies, making scientific breakthroughs, redefining artistic expression, and leveraging technology for social good, we must recognize that these victories are not just personal triumphs—they are collective milestones for all of humanity.

Education, financial independence, digital literacy, and self-belief have become the new weapons in the modern woman's arsenal. With government initiatives supporting their ambitions and an evolving society acknowledging their rightful place, there is no limit to what they can achieve. The presence of women in technology, sustainability, and governance signals that the future is not just about representation but about rightful participation in decision-making and leadership.

However, the fight is far from over. Even today, challenges persist—gender wage gaps, workplace discrimination, societal scrutiny, and the invisible burden of balancing career and family. But history has proven that every revolution starts with a few voices that refuse to be silenced. The voices of today's women are louder than ever, and they are demanding change, not as a favor but as a necessity.

To every woman reading this—whether you dream of running a business, creating art, exploring space, or simply reclaiming your right to live on your terms—know this: you are powerful beyond measure. No dream is too big, no ambition too bold. Your struggles are valid, your voice is important, and your presence in every sphere of society is invaluable.

The world is watching. The world is changing. And it is the women of today who are shaping the world of tomorrow. Rise. Lead. Inspire. The future belongs to you.

CHAPTER-17
The Silent Force – Women in Rural India

The Resilience of Rural Women in Agriculture and Industry

India's rural women form the backbone of its economy, silently driving its agricultural and industrial sectors. Even in the face of adversity, they work tirelessly in fields, factories, and small-scale industries, ensuring the sustenance of millions. Rural women constitute nearly 75% of the agricultural workforce, engaging in activities ranging from sowing and harvesting to animal husbandry and agro-processing.

Despite their immense contributions, they often remain unpaid or underpaid, their labor considered an extension of household duties rather than economic participation. Yet, their resilience is unwavering. From using traditional knowledge to manage climate change effects on crops to adopting modern organic farming techniques, these women continue to innovate and sustain rural economies.

Women are also making strides in rural industries, running dairy farms, weaving handlooms, and participating in **self-help groups (SHGs)** that manufacture everything from handicrafts to packaged foods. Government programs like Rural Livelihoods Mission and Ujjwala Yojana have played a key role in empowering them economically, helping them transition from laborers to entrepreneurs.

2. Grassroots Movements and Local Leadership

Rural women have been at the forefront of some of India's most powerful grassroots movements. From the Chipko Movement in Uttarakhand, where women hugged trees to prevent deforestation, to the anti-alcohol movements in Andhra Pradesh and Bihar, rural women have displayed unparalleled courage in demanding social change.

Women's leadership at the grassroots level has gained significant momentum, especially with the 73rd Amendment Act (1992), which reserved one-third of panchayat seats for women. This led to a surge in women sarpanches (village heads), who have since transformed governance by focusing on sanitation, education, and women's health. Notable movements include:

• **Kudumbashree (Kerala):** A women-led cooperative empowering rural women financially.

• **Self-Employed Women's Association (SEWA):** Supporting women in unorganized sectors to claim labor rights.

• **Deccan Development Society:** A network of rural Dalit women promoting sustainable agriculture and food sovereignty.

Women leaders in rural India are not just fighting for their rights but also advocating for their communities, challenging oppressive traditions, and ensuring development reaches the last mile.

Case Studies of Impactful Rural Women Leaders and Entrepreneurs

Chhavi Rajawat – The MBA Sarpanch

Chhavi Rajawat, a former corporate professional with an MBA, left her career to become the sarpanch of Soda village, Rajasthan. Through her leadership, she introduced clean drinking water, solar energy, improved roads, and digital literacy

programs, transforming the village's infrastructure.

Chetna Sinha – The Banker of Rural Women

Chetna Sinha founded the Mann Deshi Mahila Bank, India's first

bank for and by rural women. She identified the struggles of women without access to financial services and provided them with banking solutions, financial literacy, and entrepreneurship training.

Tilottama Majumdar – The Woman Reviving Dying Weaves

A handloom entrepreneur from Bengal, Tilottama Majumdar started a cooperative to revive traditional weaving techniques, giving rural women financial independence through their craft. Her efforts have provided employment to hundreds of women and kept Indian heritage alive. SHE IS ALSO A FAMOUS AUTHOR

Shyamali Khastagir – The Environmental Warrior

A tribal woman from Jharkhand, Shyamali has been leading a movement to preserve indigenous seed varieties and promote organic farming among rural women. Her work has empowered many women farmers to adopt sustainable practices.

Conclusion

The rural women of India are unsung heroines, their strength woven into the very fabric of the nation's progress.

Whether in agriculture, entrepreneurship, or governance, they continue to defy odds, creating opportunities for themselves and their communities. However, challenges remain—access to education, healthcare, and financial independence must be further strengthened.

As India moves toward a future of inclusive growth, recognizing and uplifting the silent force of rural women is not just a necessity, but a duty. With greater support, education, and investment in their potential, rural women will no longer be a silent force—they will be a driving force behind India's progress.

CHAPTER-18
Problems vs solutions
(For government to ensure- women safety)

The safety of women in India remains one of the most pressing concerns of the modern era. Despite legislative reforms, increasing awareness, and technological advancements, women across the country continue to face rampant violence, discrimination, and systemic neglect. The issue is not merely one of law enforcement but is deeply rooted in societal attitudes, cultural conditioning, and an overwhelming lack of accountability. The statistics paint a grim reality, but beyond the numbers lie the countless stories of shattered lives and lost dreams.

The Alarming Reality: Numbers That Demand Attention

Recent data from the National Crime Records Bureau (NCRB) indicates a staggering 31,677 reported cases of rape in 2021, amounting to an average of 86 rapes per day. This does not account for the numerous unreported cases where victims, out of fear of societal stigma, threats, or lack of faith in the judicial system, choose silence over justice. The conviction rate remains alarmingly low, hovering around 28%, suggesting that the vast majority of perpetrators escape punishment

However, rape is only the tip of the iceberg. Domestic violence, sexual harassment, workplace abuse, honour killings, cybercrimes, and human trafficking continue to afflict women across India. Reports suggest that 70% of Indian women face domestic violence at some point in their lives, yet a shocking 86% never seek help—a statistic that exposes the deep-rooted normalization of abuse within Indian households.

Recent Cases: The Horrors That Demand Change

While crime against women is an ongoing crisis, certain cases have recently shaken the nation and ignited public outrage.

One such case is the Kolkata Trainee Doctor Incident (August 2024), where a 31-year-old female doctor was raped and murdered within the premises of R. G. Kar Medical College and Hospital. The incident triggered massive protests across the medical community, with junior doctors striking for 42 days, demanding stringent security measures in educational and medical institutions. The case became symbolic of how even highly educated women, working in supposed 'safe spaces,' are vulnerable to such heinous crimes.

Another disturbing case surfaced in Tamil Nadu in January 2025, where authorities arrested 44 men for the systematic sexual abuse of a Dalit girl over a period of five years. The victim, who was only 13 when the abuse began, was subjected to rape by over 60 individuals, some of whom held positions of power and influence. This case shed light on the intersection of caste and gender-based violence, where marginalized women are even more vulnerable to exploitation and are often denied justice.

The Multifaceted Challenges Women Face

Women in India are not only fighting physical violence but also battling deeply ingrained societal attitudes that make justice difficult to attain.

1. Domestic Violence and Marital Rape

Domestic violence remains one of the most prevalent yet underreported crimes in India. Many women, bound by economic dependence or societal pressure, endure abuse without seeking help. Marital rape, still not criminalized in India, continues to be a major point of contention. The idea that marriage grants a husband the right to a woman's body perpetuates a culture of impunity.

2. Workplace Harassment and Unequal Treatment

Despite laws such as the Sexual Harassment of Women at Workplace Act (2013), workplace harassment continues to be rampant. Fear of losing employment, professional retaliation, or lack of support from employers prevents many women from reporting cases of harassment.

3. Human Trafficking and Forced Prostitution

India remains a hub for human trafficking, with thousands of women and girls trafficked for forced labor, domestic servitude, and sexual exploitation. The lack of proper rehabilitation programs for survivors means many are re-trafficked or forced into a life of destitution.

4. Honor Killings and Family-Controlled Violence

In many parts of India, women are still subjected to violence in the name of 'honor.' Families often resort to killing their daughters for choosing their own partners, marrying outside their caste or religion, or seeking divorce. The justification of such killings in the name of tradition continues to cost women their lives.

5. Cyber Harassment and Digital Exploitation

The rise of technology has brought with it new forms of abuse. Women face rampant cyberstalking, non-consensual sharing of intimate images, and targeted online harassment. Many victims struggle to take action due to inadequate laws and an unresponsive legal system.

The Government's Role: Initiatives for Women's Safety

In response to the increasing crimes against women, the Indian government has implemented several measures aimed at enhancing security, empowerment, and justice.

The Nirbhaya Fund, established after the brutal 2012 Delhi gang rape case, has been used to finance projects focusing on women's safety, including CCTV surveillance in public places, emergency response systems, and safety helplines. However, criticisms regarding underutilization and lack of transparency have prevented its full potential from being realized.

Several states have introduced One Stop Centres (OSCs), providing medical, legal, psychological, and police assistance to victims of gender-based violence under one roof. The Emergency Response Support System (ERSS), available nationwide through 112, offers a quick response mechanism for women in distress.

To counter sexual harassment in public transport, initiatives such as Pink Rickshaws—women-driven auto-rickshaws—and special women-only buses and metro compartments have been introduced. Additionally, safety apps such as Himmat allow women to send distress signals directly to the police.

Despite these efforts, the implementation remains a significant challenge. Many of these schemes do not reach rural areas, and corruption within the system prevents funds from being used effectively.

What More Needs to Be Done? A Roadmap for Change

While laws and policies are essential, true change requires a multifaceted approach that addresses the root causes of violence against women.

1. Changing Societal Attitudes

Education and awareness campaigns must focus on dismantling patriarchal norms that enable gender-based violence. Schools should introduce gender-sensitivity programs from an early age to ensure a progressive mindset among future generations.

2. Legal and Judicial Reforms

Fast-track courts for rape cases must be expanded, and judicial delays need to be minimized. Stricter punishments and more efficient handling of evidence collection can help improve conviction rates. Additionally, marital rape must be criminalized to grant women autonomy over their bodies.

3. Police and Law Enforcement Accountability

Many rape survivors report facing insensitivity and victim-blaming at police stations. Gender-sensitivity training for police officers, increased female representation in law enforcement, and strict action against officers who fail to handle cases properly can improve women's trust in the system.

4. Economic Empowerment and Self-Sufficiency

Financial independence is key to ensuring women are not forced to remain in abusive situations. More investment in skill development programs, microfinance initiatives, and self-help groups can help women become self-reliant.

5. Technological Interventions for Safety

Advanced AI-based security systems, smart street lighting, panic buttons in public transport, and GPS-enabled personal safety devices can enhance women's safety in urban and rural spaces.

Conclusion: A Future Where Women Feel Safe

India stands at a critical juncture. While progress has been made, the path to ensuring true safety for women remains long and arduous. This is not just a women's issue—it is a human rights issue that requires collective action from individuals, communities, policymakers, and law enforcement agencies.

Women's safety is not about restricting their movement or imposing curfews; it is about creating an environment where they can exist freely without fear. The true measure of a nation's progress lies in how it treats its women. If India aspires to be a global leader, it must start by ensuring that every woman—regardless of class, caste, or location—can live a life free from violence and fear.

The solutions exist. The question is—do we have the will to implement them?

THANKYOU!